Planting
Companions

Planting
Companions

JILL BILLINGTON

with photography by

CLIVE NICHOLS

RYLAND

PETERS

& SMALL

Dedication
To Sharon and Alan Beuthin with
gratitude and friendship

The author would like to thank the following people:
Caroline Davison for her tireless support and Geoff
Fennell for his stylish design; Clive Nichols and his
wife Jane for their continuing involvement in all
aspects of preparing the book; and Julia Brett for her
resilience and good humour in preparing the many
manifestations of the script.

First published in Great Britain in 1997
by Ryland Peters & Small
Cavendish House
51-55 Mortimer Street
London W1N 7TD

Text © 1997 Jill Billington
Design and Illustrations © 1997 Ryland Peters & Small
Photography © 1997 Ryland Peters & Small and
Clive Nichols

Produced by Mandarin Offset
Printed in Hong Kong

ISBN 1 900518 23 6

A catalogue record for this book is available from the
British Library

Senior Designer Larraine Shamwana
Designer Geoff Fennell
Project Editor Caroline Davison
Production Kate Mackillop
DTP Manager Caroline Wollen
Illustrator Liz Pepperell

Front jacket photograph (De Heurne, Holland.
Designer: Leo Nederhof)
Back jacket photograph (Hadspen House Garden and
Nursery, Somerset. Designers: Sandra and Nori Pope)

CONTENTS

AN OVERALL IMAGE

There is a human need to make our surroundings beautiful, no matter how far the wonders of technology take us. Usually the gardener's aim is a scene of planting togetherness where nothing jars, and choosing favourite plants is part of the fun. But including all of these in an allotted space is rarely possible. Every garden can be

beautiful but, unless your intentions are clear from the beginning, the process can be needlessly vexing. You can avoid this by making some basic decisions when choosing your planting companions. To this end, the book is divided into two parts. The first part considers design principles and the second looks at horticultural influences and the effects of time on planting relationships. There need be no 'mysteries' when designing with plants.

Above
Low evening light draws the eye to the parallel rhythms created by foxgloves growing among a mass of forget-me-nots (*Myosotis*).

Right
Yellow lupins and spikes of cream *Sisyrinchium striatum* are central to a composition of textured green fennel and frothy *Alchemilla mollis*.

FINDING THE RIGHT STYLE

Strolling through an art gallery shows that artists have different views of the world. Similarly, when we walk in our gardens we do not all want the same experience. Some of us look for geometric design while others enjoy seemingly artless nature. Our gardens are personal and we should ask ourselves what we want in terms of overall style, whether formal, romantic, natural or modern. Which garden image fulfils your dreams and how do you achieve it?

Formal Gardens These occur in every culture and have typical features in common: the garden spaces are simple, often composed of rectangles or parts of circles, and the whole plan is governed by geometric principles. The garden often includes permanent seats, arbours, arches or pergolas and foci such as sculpture, urns, a pool, a fountain or a well. Following the first symmetrical gardens in Egypt and the enclosed courtyard gardens of Ancient Rome, formal gardens later appeared in Italy, France and Medieval England. Some 20th-century gardens, designed by Sir Edwin Lutyens, Beatrix Farrand, Russell Page and others may be of the same formal persuasion.

Right

A formal yet romantic garden with narrow cypresses (*Cupressus*) and clipped box beside a pool is set dramatically against the landscape of southern France.

Below

This formal garden focuses on a central square surrounded by clipped golden yews, the yellow grass *Carex elata* 'Aurea' and *Alchemilla mollis*.

A sense of formality is created here by the strong central axis of the paved pathway. The overflowing foliage of the *Alchemilla mollis* and the massed white *Rosa* 'Iceberg' do not compete with the theme.

Routeways in the formal garden are well-defined, clearly indicating the direction of movement through the garden. Entrances and exits are marked with features such as twinned clipped shrubs while boundaries are marked by walls or tall, well-clipped hedging. Borders can be edged with low hedging such as common box (*Buxus sempervirens*), sweet box (*Sarcococca hookeriana humilis*), lavender (*Lavandula*) or varieties of *Santolina*.

Formal gardening will always be loved. Its simplicity is reassuring and yet, within these geometric boundaries, self-indulgence is still possible, with plants flowing in luxuriant variety. Brilliantly coloured plants and those with an untidy habit, such as shrub roses or lady's mantle (*Alchemilla mollis*), are very pleasing when grouped within a formal scheme. So, the formal garden can be planted romantically, appealing to the senses and the imagination.

Formality is not only confined to gardens with historical associations. The essential simplicity of formal designs produces an elegance or minimalism appropriate to today's buildings. Many modern designers use geometrical order to create defined spaces with ranks of repeated shapes such as box balls or elegantly tall conifers marching equally spaced across a garden, and naturally neat plants acting as sculptural full-stops.

Romantic Gardens You may prefer a romantic style, which is perhaps represented perfectly by the 'cottage garden' and firmly established in most people's minds. Gertrude Jekyll, the early 20th-century garden designer, wrote: 'They have a simple and tender charm that one may look for in vain in gardens of greater pretension.' In reality, they were more a matter of surviving from a small holding than the glorious tumble of today's cottage gardens implies. Yet the idea of abandoned ease, with roses mingling with fruit and vegetables as well as lavender and honeysuckle, appeals to everyone. The character of romantic gardens of all types clearly calls for an informal layout, often involving curved paths, hidden areas, and a sense of mystery.

References to the past are another aspect of the romantic garden style. As with the cottage garden, nostalgia is seductive, and so you may include follies, walled gardens and framed vistas. These may be festooned with climbers that mingle with clematis and roses while at foot herbaceous perennials pour forth their summer froth. The planting is insubstantial with gypsophila and fennel (*Foeniculum vulgare*) planted in drifts alongside lupins, poppies and daisy-flowered perennials as well as lush foliage patterns. The fragrance of the flowers and leaves is another ingredient of romance and there are plants that carry scent throughout the year. Night-scented flowers are especially welcome beside the house.

Light is particularly important in this context. Bright sunlight celebrates fairground colour and many vibrant flowers revel in direct sunshine. In strong light, pastels tend to lose their subtlety, thus making a case for some dappled shade where primroses, anemones and honesty provide a gleam of white and cream supported by green foliage. White flowers, however, can have enormous charm in stronger sunlight and create a highly romantic effect when allied to silver-grey foliage and pastel flower hues. Morning and evening light, which are both lower in intensity than midday sunlight, cast softer shadows and suit paler toned plants.

Left
**This small silver pear tree (*Pyrus salicifolia* 'Pendula') is the focus of a
gravelled path bordered by pink roses, *Dianthus* and *Allium cristophii*.**
Top right
**Two very old roses, the Apothecary rose (*Rosa gallica officinalis*) and striped
R. gallica 'Versicolor', are romantically associated with *Nepeta sibirica*.**
Right
**This herbaceous border contains lupins, poppies, globe thistles (*Echinops*) and
delphiniums with *Limnanthes douglasii* and *Mimulus* spilling onto the lawn.**

Natural Gardens The green movement has been gathering apace since the 'flower power' days of the Sixties although the early ideas on natural planting may be laid at the door of the Victorian gardener, William Robinson. Recently, with our reappraisal of the earth's natural riches, there has been a positive movement towards conservation and from this has grown a style of wildflower gardening that is as artistic in concept as it is horticultural.

The aim is to echo the naturalness of the countryside in our gardens, drawing on an appreciation of natural habitats. The traditional herbaceous border sites plants together purely for visual effect. Alternatively, the natural harmony achieved by linking plants from a similar environment is an ideal because the plants selected are genetically equipped to deal with the conditions as well as the contemporary need for low-maintenance gardens. If you garden in a hot, dry climate the indigenous flora will include narrow-leaved plants which thrive in those conditions while if the land is permanently damp with rich organic soil such as in a woodland garden, the planting will be thick and lush. So, working with nature and introducing plants that have a natural affinity to the conditions – an approach to gardening that we will refer to as natural compatibility – is an attractive proposition (see pages 112-31).

In the prairies, or in wildflower meadows, plants spread in drifts. The American garden designers, James van Sweden and Wolfgang Oehme, have created a new style of garden inspired by open spaces where the plants flow in simulation of nature. They simplify schemes by covering the ground with merging masses of ornamental grasses and herbaceous plants. In England, Beth Chatto's gravel garden is highly influential, indicating that working with nature can produce beautiful effects. Both of these garden styles can be adapted for the smaller city garden.

This is not to say, however, that only truly native plants should be used if you are trying to create a natural garden. Plants migrate with man and can adapt to different conditions and these new introductions will enrich local varieties. But many of these indigenous plants are invasive and compete for sunlight, water and soil. Hybrid herbaceous plants are more manageable

Inset, right

These semi-wild flowers have been skilfully yet randomly planted in long grass to create a natural, woodland effect. Among them are shade-loving *Geum* 'Borisii', *G.* 'Georgenburg', *Tradescantia* x *andersoniana* 'Zwanenburg Blue' and the pinkish-purple flower spikes of *Gladiolus communis byzantinus*, an early summer-flowering corm.

Above

This large garden creates a very natural look and is dependent upon foliage rather than flowers. Acers and azaleas provide brilliant colour in the autumn.

Main picture, left

A woodland path curves along the base of an ancient moat and is sensitively planted with masses of *Scilla bithynica* that have naturalized over the years.

and often more ornate, and so there is an advantage to using them. Disease-resistant hybrids can also be used although choosing non-native plants for the natural garden requires a certain degree of knowledge as well as a sensitive eye. But if you ensure that the plants you choose are all naturally compatible then you will create a natural garden style that suggests the wild without the actuality.

Trees and shrubs should not be omitted when referring to a natural style of garden, the colours of autumn fruits and leaves being firm reminders of the countryside. Like herbaceous plants, varieties can be an improvement on the species from which they came. Birches and rowans, for example, can be associated with shrubs such as dogwoods (*Cornus*) and species roses. If each group has common ecological needs then they will look charming and attractive together and suggest the countryside even in the city.

13

The Late 20th Century Since the end of the last century, garden designers have started to turn away from geometric bedding schemes, preferring to emulate the randomness of nature. Indeed, in the United States and in Europe, plants are now less formally arranged on a 'grid basis' and native plants are mixed in with garden cultivars. The plants are combined with a sympathetic understanding of their natural requirements and self-sustaining schemes are thus created that stabilize after a few years, filled with plants that tolerate the same growing conditions.

The plant communities are constructed in drifting flows or, if the plants are naturally 'clumped', they are allowed to reach their ultimate spread without being overcrowded by dense planting numbers. Some plants, such as the tall, rhythmical verbascums and veronicastrums and static masses like

Main picture, left
Eupatorium purpureum, Veronicastrum virginicum album and ***Atriplex hortensis rubra*** here dominate pale phlox, monarda and silver artemisia.
Inset, left
Pink ***Echinacea purpurea*** 'Magnus' are attractive among these grasses including the slim ***Calamagrostis*** x ***acutiflora*** 'Karl Foerster'.

Above
Silver-white flowers of ***Artemisia*** 'Jim Russell' have been combined with pink ***Monarda*** 'Cherokee' and dark plum-purple ***Atriplex hortensis rubra***.
Left
Wine-red ***Angelica gigas*** stands out here among ***Monarda*** 'Purple Ann', ***M.*** 'Oudolf's Charm', ***Deschampsia*** 'Gold Tan' and ***Miscanthus sinensis*** 'Flamingo'.

geraniums become building blocks with more fluid ornamental grasses incorporated to create movement. In short, the plants are well-spaced, relaxed and content. As well as creating effects that take form, space, colour and movement into account, this approach also exploits changing light levels with plants back- or side-lit to reveal sensuous silhouettes and patterns.

Plants are not regimented with the largest at the back and the smallest ranked at the front. Instead, you often have to look through tall plants, such as *Verbena bonariensis*, to see the plant details beyond, the images filtering through the 'transparent' plants in the foreground. As the seasons pass the plants shift in dominance. So astrantias or poppies give way to *Macleaya cordata* or phlox and plantains. Many of the plants that die earlier in the season remain in place, just as they would in the wild, which means that seed-heads and parchment-like grasses also provide frosted winter effects.

On the other hand, plants can travel the shrinking world as easily as we do so that we can grow subtropical plants even in temperate countries. Exotic plants in any country are really those that would not survive without man's interference. Thus, a grove of eucalyptus may thrive in the Scottish Hebrides and a lotus may flower on Long Island in the United States.

The use of hard materials, such as plastic, glass, timber and gravel, is also being explored in modern gardens. Artists are making gardens and they are prepared to try anything, from symbolism to poetry, from new materials to new technology. An exploitation of the senses, using the textures, shapes and colours of plants, is leading us towards gardens for the 20th century.

Left
This garden celebrates the details of succulent aeoniums, agaves, echeverias, aloes, ixias and watsonias in contrast with phormiums and grassy dierama.
Right
A harmonious minimalist scheme includes surface materials of gravel and timber that emphasize elegant maples, clipped box and grasses.
Below
Sculptured form rather than intricate detail creates a simple effect. Lavender, santolina and mossy saxifrage lie low beneath *Acer grosseri*.

Modern Gardens As the new millennium approaches, it is interesting to see how garden design has altered during this century and in what direction it is going. It seems that people are reluctant to leave behind classical images even though respect for the past can result in mere pastiches. There is also much interest in restoring historical gardens although plant accuracy is not easy or even necessary. Why use a weak plant when there are stronger new versions that would most certainly have been used had the plant been available at the time? History may have presented us with a legacy of magnificent gardens but creativity does not simply come to a full-stop. The popularity of the natural garden style shows how much planting ideas have changed since the formal bedding schemes of the last century. We now accept ecological responsibility.

Travel opens up other possibilities, enabling ideas to be caught in a wider net than in the past. For example, in terms of garden philosophy, the influence of classical Japanese gardens has been considerable. The simplicity of these gardens is admired: plants do not jostle in overcrowded flummery and on occasion plants such as santolina can be clipped to take on the role of sculpture and combined with natural materials like gravel, stone and moss.

PLANTING FOR
VISUAL EFFECT

FORM AND SHAPE

Ordering a personal outdoor space depends greatly upon the structures used. Plants can be as effective as hard materials for dividing spaces and enclosing areas, providing a solid mass that can be carved like stone into architectural form. But there are also plants with a naturally strong shape, requiring no assistance from man,

which gives them great character. Some plants such as exotic fan palms stand out as powerfully as monoliths, individual and eye-catching while others, including irises and hostas, may not be prima donnas but possess a stylish, natural growth habit. These plant shapes are invaluable because they prevent the scene from becoming bland. If there were no structure to the planting the garden would be as confused as melody without rhythm.

Left

A weeping *Pyrus salicifolia* 'Pendula' flanked by two box spheres beside an angular knot garden formally dominates the other plant shapes.

Above

This symmetrical garden with standard roses trained as 'drumsticks' depends upon clipped mounds of lavender and santolina for its effect.

THE ROLE OF FORM AND SHAPE

Plant shapes are as diverse as all living things but some grow with an expressive natural habit that affects the ambience of the garden. Using them well ensures harmony, emphasizes depth and creates illusions of scale in the garden.

People tend to regard colour as the primary concern of planting schemes. I believe that the form of a plant should be considered first. Early photographs of Gertrude Jekyll borders, taken in her garden at Munstead Wood, in England, show her understanding of form as the foundation of mixed planting. She is respected as a colourist but many of her favourite plants had exceptional form as well. She used the distinctive shapes of lilies, delphiniums, tree lupins (*Lupinus arboreus*) and hollyhocks (*Alcea rosea*) to add stature to her plant groups. In fact, a black-and-white photograph would show clearly how very attractive a border of mixed plants can be even without the colour. I rest my case.

Different plant forms and shapes have a particular impact on a group of plants or on a border. The narrow vertical shapes used by Gertrude Jekyll, such as conifers, tall grasses and erect bamboos as well as flower spikes are very noticeable in mixed schemes (see pages 30-31). These plant shapes attract the eye, making static

Above
Variegated *Cornus alternifolia* 'Argentea' spreads widely above the mounding, large, sculptured, blue leaves of *Hosta sieboldiana elegans*.
Left
Irish junipers (*Juniperus communis* 'Hibernica') are here associated with other shapes including *Ligustrum ovalifolium* 'Aureum' standards and weeping *Prunus* x *yedoensis* 'Shidare-yoshino'.

statements that simply demand attention. When viewed from a distance, they become arresting perpendiculars that link land with sky. Narrow vertical forms, such as the rather grand foxtail lily (*Eremurus robustus*), red-hot pokers (*Kniphofia*) and *Persicaria bistorta*, also provide a focus or resting point so that there is a pause for a while.

The form of a plant may also direct attention horizontally, growing parallel to the plane of the landscape while being at right angles to the upright forms. *Viburnum plicatum* 'Mariesii' is a classic of this type, being layered in horizontally growing branches, an effect that is accentuated still further when the flat-headed, lacecap flowers

Above
Acer palmatum Dissectum Viride Group has a
mounded form against which the neat spheres of
Allium hollandicum and the pink poker-like flowers
of **Persicaria bistorta** 'Superba' look effective.
Right
The tall, upright habit of a dark green yew **Taxus
baccata** 'Fastigiata' is echoed in the foreground by
the upright flower spikes of **Kniphofia** 'Goldelse'.

These act as a relief among the more amorphous foliage of other plants as well as making sense of a confusion of foliar textures in which there is too much dependency upon colour.

The round forms of plants such as cistus and artemisia create a feeling of stability; they are the anchors in the garden (see pages 38-39). In formal gardens they are used as twin markers, say clipped box domes, on either side of a path or to acknowledge an entrance. In more fluid planting schemes they supply pauses that earth the dynamism of tumbling plants and, grouped as repeat shapes, they create an undulating rhythm. Weeping shapes are similarly mound-like but they also suggest movement in their downward flow to the ground (see pages 34-35). Their relationship to the horizontal plane is never better seen than when a huge weeping willow trails downward to a surface plane of water.

So, as we will see later, the general mingling of plants is greatly improved by including very shapely ones to act as accents. Careful consideration is necessary, however, because using a great number of striking plants can result in a rather restless look. Fortunately, the majority of plants do not have such demanding forms and act as neutral buffers, as valuable in a mass of plants as a chorus line around the main players.

appear in late spring. The horizontal habit is just as common in nature as the vertical one but the effect created is quite different (see pages 32-33). The eye does not rest but is taken across the width of the view, then possibly bounced back by a similar shape on the far side.

Sword-like leaf shapes, such as yuccas, add drama to the garden while the simple elegance of irises, ornamental grasses, fanned sisyrinchiums and flowing daylilies (*Hemerocallis*) provide a far quieter chorus (see pages 36-37). Grouped in clumps or drifts, plants with lance-shaped or strap-like leaves, such as the yellow flag iris (*Iris pseudacorus*), also provide clear, linear patterns.

GROUPING FORMS AND SHAPES

Many plants, such as sword palms, agaves, cacti and yuccas, have a high profile both literally and artistically, acting as a focus, rather like sculpture in a gallery. These individuals brook very little interference. However, narrow upright plants are often too thin to be sited alone. They act as full-stops and take the eye upwards which can make isolated specimens look awkward. If you think of statuary in many cities of the world, the single pillar is rarely successful. For this reason, these plants look more secure as part of a group.

When combining plants, there are certain principles to bear in mind, which we shall consider in turn. Narrow verticals, for example, can be repeated on a different scale in other areas of the garden to echo the form and create visual links. Alternatively, a group of the same plant growing together makes the total mass wider and therefore visually more stable. Or, differently shaped plants can be grown at foot that have a horizontal, rounded or weeping habit to anchor the perpendicular shape to the ground.

Grouping By Number As I have already said, one specimen becomes a focus but if there are two similar specimens, however far apart they are, the focus becomes the centre of the imagined line that connects the pair. In other words, the eye does not switch constantly from one to the other but chooses to rest halfway between the two. This is why identical plants are so often selected to act as flanking sentinels to draw the attention to some important feature like an entrance or a seat. If you do not want this to happen, then a third doppelganger should be planted within the same scene. So what happens then?

To an observer, groups of three objects always unite to make a triangle, which is a stable, pleasing shape, whether equilateral or not. So planting a group of three Irish junipers (*Juniperus communis* 'Hibernica') or silver birches provides a satisfactory focal group. In the same way, a group of three shrubs such as *Cornus alba* varieties or shrub roses look attractive, however the triangular form is distributed. This applies equally to many herbaceous

Below
Four neat cone shapes of clipped box shrubs add definition to a stone square while antique pansies planted in the central bed provide pattern and colour.

Below
Asymmetrically planted vertical forms of *Carnegiea gigantea* have been echoed elsewhere to balance their impact and draw attention to the agaves and aloes.

groups such as clumps of poppies or hostas. On the other hand, a group of three dissimilar plants may also be satisfactorily grouped to form a pyramid. This is a classic style of grouping involving one tall plant, like a fastigiate form of rosemary (*Rosmarinus officinalis*), with a rounded shrub such as a potentilla at the base and a spreading plant, perhaps *Cotoneaster horizontalis*, to ground the scheme.

As soon as you increase the number to four the eye gets up to its old tricks of trying to divide even numbers in half and then half again to make sense of them. This phenomenon can be overcome by planting in odd numbers because the random shapes made by the grouped plants cannot easily be turned into mathematical patterns. So, a group of five plants would need one dominant overseer, perhaps a small tree such as *Aralia elata*, then two mounds of *Viburnum davidii* plus a wider plant of medium height like *Acer palmatum dissectum* and a spreading, ground level plant such as *Juniperus horizontalis* to act as an anchor.

If you want a much larger scheme remember the organized left-hand side of your brain, which is trying to unscramble the mass of plants into groups and patterns. The key is to recognize the dominant plants first and then to link them loosely into relationships of odd numbers. Look for plants that have similarities of form or colour and, knowing that these too will be connected in your mind's eye, continue to work them in as uneven number groups, some larger and some smaller. The moment you use a pair of plants you reintroduce the tension between the two, suggesting division, formality and even symmetry. The only exception to these general rules on grouping is when you deliberately create a geometric garden design in which you have to use an even number of plants.

These ideas on grouping plants by number are intended to make planning easier but I must add that many plants do not obey such tidy rules. Nature is wayward and suckering plants and surface-rooting perennials, for example, will behave as they like. They have no number skills.

Below
A low line of hostas densely planted with the shrub *Rosa* x *francofurtana* link together to form a compact triangular relationship.

Below
Massed succulents, *Agave parryi huachucensis*, *Senecio mandraliscae*, *Colletia paradoxa* and *Puya coerulea violacea* jostle for space on this raised bank.

Grouping Through Repetition Visitors to a garden make associations by eye all the time, often unconsciously. Only when presented with an 'all-over' design, such as a wildflower meadow, does this not happen. Then people talk of 'carpets' of flowers. This by implication means a flat, two-dimensional decoration like tapestry. For this reason, planting in one plane, such as a row of equally spaced trees or infilling parterre with the same plant, can have great charm.

Repeat planting need not be this formal, however. Among the froth of flowers clearly defined leaf shapes, such as phormiums or cannas, will always be noticeable. Repeated randomly in these garden simple shapes will be picked up by the eye and create rhythmical relationships. The invaluable *Viburnum davidii*, for example, with its mound-forming habit, can be sited in different areas, sometimes in threes, and maybe on its own. Above head height, a mop-head acacia such as *Robinia pseudoacacia* 'Inermis' will echo the roundness and elsewhere *Cistus* x *hybridus* (syn. *C.* x *corbariensis*) will follow through.

Strongly shaped leaves have the same effect. Tall sword-like crocosmias and phormiums as well as reedy plants and grasses relate through inference. These plants create a sense of unity in the garden even across an expanse of water as do the erect flower heads of lupins, kniphofias

Top left

A meandering path is lined by phlox, *Saponaria* x *lempergii* 'Max Frei' and *Astrantia major* 'Claret' as well as *Macleaya cordata*, *Atriplex hortensis rubra* and *Angelica archangelica*.

Left

Dominatingly erect, sword-like phormium foliage and iris leaves make linear patterns that are in vertical contrast with the flat surface of water.

and delphiniums, standing distinctively among their peers and duplicating one another in shape. Creating plant patterns is described in 'The Rhythm of Repeats', on pages 58-59.

Repeating plant shapes is also an invaluable means of emphasizing a change of direction along a sinuous path. You create logical reasons for the turns by planting shrubs or perennials on either side. I suggest using similarly shaped or identical plants because there is already enough happening with the twists and turns of the path.

The repetition of shapes need not involve the same type of plant or even be on the same scale. For example, you could plant a fastigiate tree within the same frame as a group of foxgloves. These relationships work well because one plant flatters the other. Much can be achieved simply by observing the different shapes of plants and seeing what characteristics they share.

Distance and Perspective Instant perspective can be created using the classic avenue of trees viewed from one end. Most private gardens are not large enough for this effect but it is possible to increase the sense of spaciousness by repeating plant shapes, such as bamboos and grasses, across the width and depth of the garden. You can also increase the illusion of depth by ensuring that the specimens near the house are not only similar in shape but different in size. So, a group of tall conifers like the fastigiate yew (*Taxus baccata* 'Fastigiata') nearest to the viewer could be imitated by a distant group of smaller conifers such as *Juniperus communis* 'Sentinel'.

A similar result can be achieved by using larger shrubs and herbaceous perennials with distinctive forms close to the main viewpoint and then echoing the shapes further away in progressively smaller detail. The whole effect may be heightened, narrowing the boundaries with distance and using less distinct plant shapes further away, or by using colours that become paler and bluer in retreat. Such tricks have been used by painters for centuries. Even clipped hedges, repeated closely one behind the other, suggest a greater distance between them than is the case.

Another trick used for centuries is to 'borrow' the landscape, a technique known in Japan as *shakkei*. The aim is to link the cultivated garden with the environment beyond. In classical times, the distant view would be linked to the garden by framing it with selected plants. In much smaller gardens the shape of the plants beyond the garden can be imitated, thus setting up a link that goes beyond the physical boundaries and greatly increasing the apparent depth of the garden.

Without stretching my credibility, I would like to compare designing with plants to a well-organized game of football. The teamwork depends upon the individuals knowing not only where the ball is but also the position of each player, and passing the ball forward and back. In the garden, the eye may be regarded as the ball, and the more striking plants as the players, so that the viewer looks from plant to plant while never losing sight of the unity of the whole.

Top right
These rhythmical wave-like forms of hedging help to define the width of the garden while also suggesting the conclusion of the garden space.
Right
In this garden, the boundary definition is far from distinct. A semi-transparent fence enables the wheat field and distant trees beyond the garden to be 'borrowed' and become part of the scene.

Grouping Through Contrast So far I have not talked of the value of contrasting plant shapes in any detail. If everything in a garden is predictable and there are no contrasts between spaces and masses or between light and dark areas, or if the planting is too even-tempered then the result is disappointingly bland. Only through contrast is the overall effect heightened, resulting in an atmospheric garden that stirs the emotions.

Planting is enlivened by contrast. The habit of the dogwood (*Cornus*), for example, is to reach upwards, creating a bowl-like profile that can be settled at foot by the tiered layers of *Juniperus sabina* 'Tamariscifolia' while the horizontal *J. x media* 'Pfitzeriana' provides an ideal contrast to the upright swords of phormiums or yuccas.

Rather less dramatically, many herbaceous plants point to the sky and stand out among their more casual peers. The vertical *Salvia x superba*, for instance, looks all the more striking rising from the rounded mounds of the daisy-flowered *Anthemis punctata cupaniana*. Alternatively, red spires of lupins are enhanced by the flat-headed yarrows (*Achillea*). Similarly, the soft, flattened flower heads of sedums will anchor the swaying grasses or the perpendicular foliage of phormiums firmly to the ground.

Left
Implied links between repeated grass-like forms such as *Pennisetum alopecuroides*, *Cortaderia selloana* 'Pumila', *Miscanthus floridulus* and stark *Phormium tenax* are levelled by the sedums planted lower down in the bed.
Top right
Horizontal layering is characteristic of *Viburnum plicatum* 'Mariesii'. The tiers of flowers lie in layers while below the massed, vertical, candle-like flowers of *Persicaria* provide a contrast.

As well as drawing your attention to the habit of a plant, contrast is also a very good means of creating tension in the garden. Some shapes, such as perpendiculars, are always the boss and dominate a plant group while evergreens such as viburnums have a solidity to their mass that contrasts wonderfully with delicately structured perennials. The heavy, cabbage-like leaves of the herbaceous perennial *Crambe cordifolia* make it difficult to site. Paradoxically the flowers themselves provide a contrast, being hazy rather like a giant gypsophila. *Salvia pratensis* with its mass of fine, pale lavender flower spikes, is also an ideal companion. The feathery appearance of *Solidago* flowers can also be used to offset the powerful, rounded leaves of the bergenia family.

Not all plant forms are so distinctive and many gardeners include fragile-looking plants like grasses and fennel to contrast with other strong foliage shapes. Similarly, the hazy flowers of sea lavender (*Limonium*) look superb with the spiky leaves and flowers of *Eryngium bourgatii*. (For further suggestions on using unstructured forms see 'Using Visual Textures', on pages 54-57.) Clearly, contrast as a means of heightening experience is a valuable tool – did Beauty lose her looks when the Beast redeemed his?

Centre left
The strikingly uncompromising, spiky form of a static *Cordyline australis* is echoed by the lupins while the flat-headed flowers of *Achillea* 'Coronation Gold' layer in counterpoint.
Left
Tall, elegant, yellow flower spikes of *Ligularia* 'The Rocket' and the leaves of *Phormium tenax* Purpureum Group create powerfully vertical forms which contrast effectively with the flowing, brown sedge grass at the front of the border.

THE DIFFERENT FORMS AND SHAPES

The variety of plant forms offered to us by nature is a continual spur to the imagination but it would be useful at this stage to name names, looking at those plants with a distinctive shape and at how they can be used when designing your garden.

Using Narrow Vertical Plants An exclamation mark makes the reader pause and narrow vertical forms have exactly the same effect in the garden. They are perhaps the most prominent of

Chamaecyparis lawsoniana 'Columnaris Glauca', black *Taxus baccata* 'Fastigiata' and the greyish Irish juniper (*Juniperus communis* 'Hibernica').

Deciduous trees such as pale pink *Prunus* 'Amanogawa' and the crab apple *Malus* 'Van Eseltine' also have a slimline habit with the added benefits of flower power, autumn leaf colour and attractive fruiting. Many tree varieties are so tall and slim that they add a basso profondo drama to the scene. The Lombardy poplar (*Populus nigra italica*), which is often repeated to

form a wind-break, is a familiar image in France. When searching for sentinel trees look for the words 'Columnare', 'Erecta', 'Spire' and 'Fastigiata'. They focus the attention when grown as single specimens and can be used in groups to form a boundary or an avenue.

On a much smaller scale, vertical forms can be echoed across the beds and borders. Many herbaceous plants have a stylish perpendicular power. Lythrum, lupins, acanthus, veratrum and kniphofia all stand out in summer's lush disarray.

the plant forms, making sense of an otherwise restless garden scene and acting as focal points whatever the seasonal disarray.

In Mediterranean climates the Italian cypress (*Cupressus sempervirens* 'Stricta') dominates the countryside but there are many other conifers with a narrow vertical habit (otherwise known as fastigiate) such as the gracious incense cedar (*Calocedrus decurrens*). Smaller conifers that are suitable for modest gardens include the blueish

Above left
These flowers with a naturally erect habit include *Papaver orientale* 'Patty's Plum', *Iris* 'Shampoo' and *Allium bollandicum* 'Purple Sensation'.
Above centre
The eye-catching supremacy of *Cupressus sempervirens* is unbeaten among tall narrow trees; even the sculpture is subservient.
Above right
Massed peonies, veronicas and a lightly clipped standard willow tree are dominated here by the dark, narrow and upright form of an Irish juniper.

Planted in groups they create visual links across the garden that reinforce the sense of order and produce maximum decorative impact. Few are as tall as the biennial *Verbascum bombyciferum* whose spires reach 2 m (6½ ft) tall. Many hybrid delphiniums are even taller, their heavily flowering columns snapping unless securely staked. Late in the season, *Cimicifuga ramosa* is a challenger with its branching cream flower spikes that reach 1.5 m (5 ft). Do not neglect the foxglove in shaded areas or *Ligularia* 'The Rocket' where the soil is damp.

These vertical plants are very dominant so dilute their power with other massed verticals such as *Veronicastrum virginicum* (syn. *Veronica virginica*) at a lower level. Other good associates include the softer *Stachys byzantina*, layering hostas, round-leaved heucheras and mounding geraniums. In hot sun, artemisias may mellow austere kniphofias and in shade feathery astilbe leaves and ferns may act as foils for foxgloves.

Above
This colourful combination of *Lythrum salicaria* 'Lady Sackville' and *Lysimachia ephemerum* with their strongly vertical habit is accentuated by the *Berberis thunbergii* 'Rose Glow' which provides a suitable backdrop of purple and pink.
Right
Massed erect flower spikes in a herbaceous bed are overseen by tall, lilac delphiniums at the back. In the foreground there are layers of lupins, salvias, erysimum and silver-foliaged stachys which serve to duplicate the vertical forms.

Using Horizontal Plants The horizontal line is less demanding of attention than the vertical but is an invaluable means of leading the eye around the garden. You can avoid simply leading the viewer's eye nowhere by ensuring that it meets either a place of rest or a suggestion of hidden mystery. This dynamism can be achieved by duplicating plants that have a horizontal habit in different sites.

widely. *C. kousa*, although not horizontally tiered, has flat flower heads or bracts which are upturned along the branches in early summer. So even fine details can echo the habit of other plants.

Lacecap hydrangeas and viburnums also have flat flower heads that suggest a layering effect. The whole habit of *Viburnum plicatum* 'Mariesii' is in fact horizontally branched while white *Hydrangea macro-*

Above
Known as the 'wedding cake tree' *Cornus controversa* is valued for its naturally layered habit.

The horizontal line is evident at all heights from the great cedar *Cedrus libani atlantica* 'Glauca' and the more modest Scots pine (*Pinus sylvestris*) down to the delightful, earth-bound carpets of recumbent junipers and mat-forming thymes. There are other particularly beautiful trees of which *Cornus controversa* 'Variegata' is the most outstanding. It is layered in tiers, reaches 15 m (50 ft) tall and stretches just as

Above
Elegantly structured *Viburnum plicatum* 'Pink Beauty' carries its flowers in layered, parallel horizontals.

phylla 'Veitchii', *H. m*. 'Blue Wave' and dark pink *H. m*. 'Geoffrey Chadbund' are well known for their horizontal effect. Another strongly horizontal shrub is *Prunus laurocerasus* 'Zabeliana' which grows more or less anywhere and stretches as wide as 2.5 m (8 ft) while being only half that height. It provides a perfect foil for perpendicular foxgloves and fanning ferns. They look wonderful together.

Some smaller shrubs also perform in this way, spreading wide branches parallel to the earth for about 60-90 cm (2-3 ft). They include the evergreen *Lonicera pileata* and *Cotoneaster horizontalis*, a deciduous shrub with flowers and berries. Both have tiny leaves and form decorative underskirts beneath larger shrubs. The witch hazels (*Hamamelis*) are also wide-spreading, producing a rich perfume from their

HORIZONTAL PLANTS

***Prunus laurocerasus* 'Zabeliana'**
An evergreen with glossy leaves and candle-like flowers. It grows to 1.2 m (4 ft) with a spread of 2.5 m (8 ft).

***Sedum* 'Herbstfreude'**
An herbaceous perennial with a height and spread of 60 cm (2 ft), pink or red flower heads and glaucous foliage.

often be grown as an elegant specimen with rhododendrons, skimmias and pieris in undulating acidic woodland. The maples in the smaller Dissectum Group have a softly layered habit that looks beautiful trailing over walls or arching over water.

The horizontal line is highly influential in planting design. It is a leveller, taking the eye sideways and presenting other plants much as a plinth supports

Above
A magnificent specimen of an aged *Juniperus* x *media* 'Pfitzeriana' shows a clearly horizontal habit.

yellow to orange winter flowers while the floriferous *Genista pilosa* 'Lemon Spreader', which has yellow flowers in late summer, stretches as wide as 1.2-1.5 m (4-5 ft); both prefer acidic soil.

A word here about the palmate Japanese maples (*Acer*). They are not literally horizontal but many of them have a genteel, wide-spreading habit, particularly in maturity. *Acer palmatum atropurpureum* can

***Taxus baccata* 'Dovastoniana'**
A yew tree with a horizontal habit of tiered branches that often spread very wide indeed. It grows up to 1.2 m (4 ft) tall with a spread of 2.5 m (8 ft).

***Viburnum plicatum* 'Mariesii'**
A flowering deciduous shrub with a wide-spreading habit. The flat white florets that form the flowers appear in late spring and early summer and lie up-turned along the branches. It grows to a height of 1.8 m (6 ft) with a spread of 2.5 m (8 ft).

Above
Achillea 'Coronation Gold' contrasts strikingly with *Ligularia* 'The Rocket' and *Heuchera* 'Palace Purple'.

sculpture. On this basis, a mass of bergenias and hostas set off astilbe flower spikes to perfection. In the same way, flat-headed flowers such as the achilleas, ice-plants (*Sedum spectabile*), the plateau heads of heleniums and many species of chrysanthemum echo the horizontal line of shrubs elsewhere in the garden and add a reassuring flatness that will also complement a level sweep of lawn.

Using Weeping Plants The role of weeping forms in the garden is particularly interesting. Although they can be quite static shapes, rather like upturned mops, most weeping plants are in fact movers and shakers, bringing movement and vitality to the garden scene. The weeping willow *Salix* x *sepulcralis chrysocoma* drifts in the wind, a flowing motion characteristic of several weeping plants. The much smaller Young's weeping birch (*Betula pendula* 'Youngii') adds great charm

Betula pendula 'Tristis', for example, and the Swedish birch (*B. p.* 'Dalecarlica') have an elegant but drooping habit. When placed in groups, from three upwards, they have a settling influence on both country or city gardens.

Many trees have weeping varieties including weeping ash, weeping golden beech and trailing robinia. A word of warning about the weeping cherries: many are grafted on to other trees. The trunk of the ice-cream-pink *Prunus* 'Kanzan'

'Shirotae'), with its fragrant, double white flowers, whose branches trail to the ground with age. It spreads to 8 m (26 ft) in diameter and is often used as a specimen because there is little room beneath it for anything other than very low herbaceous plants or small spring-flowering bulbs.

While discussing trees I should mention conifers, many of which have a stylish habit. These include the blue Atlantic cedar (*Cedrus libani atlantica* 'Glauca Pendula') and Brewer's spruce

Above
Bushily evergreen *Itea ilicifolia* has attractive, glossy, dark green leaves but is also valued for its long trails of catkin-like racemes in late summer.

Above
***Pyrus salicifolia* 'Pendula', the pretty weeping ornamental pear, has narrow, silver-grey leaves. It is deciduous and has white flowers in the spring.**

Above
This *Prunus* 'Kiku-shidare-zakura', which is also known as 'Cheal's Weeping Cherry', has been planted here with clipped box and stiff yuccas.

to the shrub garden where plants like rhododendrons and pieris look like static mounds in acidic, semi-woodland conditions. It works equally well enlivening heavier evergreens such as viburnums or the Portugal laurel (*Prunus lusitanica*).

Some of the other silver birches look particularly effective when grouped. The sadly named

grows to an enormous width while the original tree retains a modest height so the branches fountain awkwardly from the trunk like flowers stuffed thoughtlessly into a vase. The ungrafted *P. subhirtella* 'Pendula Rubra' is far more graceful in habit. I also have a penchant for another semi-weeping relative, the Mount Fuji cherry (*P.*

(*Picea breweriana*) whose arched arms carry trailing branchlets in a balletic manner. They also cohabit contentedly with all acid-loving plants such as heaths and provide a foil for many other flowering shrubs, from weigelas and fuchsias to roses of all kinds. A tree for smaller gardens is the weeping silver pear (*Pyrus salicifolia* 'Pendula') whose gentle movement has real vitality. Its soft, grey foliage blends well with silver-leaved and herbaceous planting and with roses.

The more modest shrub *Buddleja alternifolia* has a downward-flowing charm. When trained upon a single stem, it produces arching trails covered in lilac flowers in early summer. Growing to a height of 3 m (10 ft) with a span of nearly 4 m (13 ft), it can be grown as a single specimen or to back a border in a mixed scheme.

dramatically with plants of a more wispy nature such as grasses, gypsophila or artemisias. The small tree *Cotoneaster* 'Hybridus Pendulus' also has a stiff weeping structure when grafted on to a stem. It adds formal distinction to rampant planting and can be used as a focal point like the fastigiate plants just described (see page 30).

The weeping character is less dominant at the herbaceous level. Some naturally arching plants, such as acid-loving *Gentiana asclepiadea*

or *Fuchsia* 'Cascade', are well suited to raised banks because their trailing habit is best seen from below. They look attractive with the weeping conifers such as *Cedrus deodara* 'Golden Horizon' or *Tsuga canadensis* 'Pendula' and with the downward-flowing style of smaller acers.

Below
This young *Cedrus libani atlantica* 'Pendula' has a distinctive weeping form. It is planted here with *Pseudolarix amabilis* and a prostrate juniper.

Above
The trailing golden racemes of laburnum have made it a popular garden tree. Here it is associated with wistaria, alliums and *Alchemilla mollis*.

Not all weeping plants have this charismatic movement. The weeping purple beech (*Fagus sylvatica* 'Purpurea Pendula') has a height and spread of 3 m (10 ft), producing an unshiftable mound of bronze-black leaves on rigidly weeping branches. This immovability provides an ideal backdrop for stiff phormiums and contrasts

Using Spiky and Grass-Shaped Plants

Shrubs and herbaceous plants with grass-like foliage share the same differences as weeping plants. Stiff cacti, for example, are resolutely stationary whereas ornamental grasses possess elegantly recurved leaves that catch the light and are responsive to wind. These plants also come in all sizes from stately bamboos to tiny *Armeria juniperifolia*. They all play a part when associated sympathetically with other plants.

Larger plants such as cordylines and yuccas are usually static. Their immobile resemblance to sculpture inevitably attracts attention. You can reduce their impact by pairing them in formal opposition, by grouping them in the mass or by siting them with equally provocative shapes such as agaves, palms, clivias and aloes in hotter climes or with *Trachycarpus fortunei*, *Melianthus major*, *Acanthus spinosus*, *Eryngium agavifolium* or *Macleaya cordata* if hardiness is an issue.

Other sword-like herbaceous plants have this static character but they are more manageable and merge within a softer garden scheme. They include *Sisyrinchium striatum*, the crocosmias, *Astelia nervosa* and some spiky kniphofias. To emphasize the vertical form of these perennials they should be combined with the giant reed (*Arundo donax*) or with inflexible grasses such as

Top left

Beautiful pink thalictrum is highly conspicuous but combines beautifully with ornamental grasses such as *Carex muskingumensis*, *Calamagrostis* as well as *Briza maxima*.

Left

The softly recurving foliage of this pampas grass, *Cortaderia selloana* 'Aureolineata', flows luxuriously over the yellow-and-red *Potentilla* 'William Rollison and *P.* 'Yellow Queen'.

the blue oat grass (*Helictotrichon sempervirens*, syn. *Avena candida*), blue *Leymus arenarius* (syn. *Elymus arenarius*) and the feather reed grass (*Calamagrostis* x *acutiflora* 'Stricta').

These plants are also invaluable in mixed herbaceous beds, sorting out the confusion of miscellaneous foliage and flower patterns. In summer, when there is much to excite the eye, the spiky, jade-green leaves of the *Iris germanica* hybrids have a calming effect on a sunny border. The elegant swords of *I. pseudacorus*, reaching up to 1.2 m (4 ft) high, look magnificent above damp-loving plants such as hostas, astilbes, ligularias and primulas. They are also effective with rodgersias, rheums and cimicifugas, and can compete with the huge paddle-shaped leaves of the skunk cabbage (*Lysichiton americanus*) or the jagged-leaved *Gunnera manicata*.

The more modest *Iris pallida* has a distinctive fan-shaped form that must be displayed with some care because the leaves are quite two-dimensional. It is best planted in parallel groups and not obscured by a flummery of foliage. The variegated forms are the best. *Iris pallida* 'Argentea Variegata' is white with dove-grey colouring while *I. p.* 'Variegata' has more cream-gold variegation. Both look effective in front of the dark or massed foliage of shrubs or herbaceous planting.

Less sculptural, but simpler to blend with other plants, are the reedy leaf shapes that move and catch the light. A good choice is one of the coloured varieties of *Iris sibirica* whose fine leaves emerge as a mass of arching reeds and reach about 90 cm (3 ft) tall. They associate well with moisture-loving plants such as the yellow flag iris (*I. pseudacorus*) and the variegated, curvaceous grass *Glyceria maxima* 'Variegata'.

A versatile plant for many garden styles is the daylily (*Hemerocallis*) whose shiny, reed-like leaves may be merged within an herbaceous mixture or massed with shrubs, girdling or weaving among them. *Libertia formosa* is nearly as useful but requires a sunny site. Its simple white flower spikes and shiny, arching, grass-like form look well among the brocaded textures of other plants. The clivias and agapanthus with strap-like leaves can be grown in association with other herbaceous perennials but their decorative foliage also makes an effective ground cover.

If you want tall, flowing foliage consider the Amur silver grass (*Miscanthus sacchariflorus*) that grows to 2 m (6½ ft) tall from ground level every year and the less hardy 4.5 m (15 ft) tall *Arundo donax*. Both are architectural, upright plants that give structure to wide herbaceous beds. *M. sinensis* varieties also form large clumps of arching leaves that rustle in the breeze. Some sympathetic associates are other grasses that undulate in a satisfactory manner, such as the evergreen sedge *Carex oshimensis* 'Variegata', grown in an ornamental grass bed. The fragile-looking *Milium effusum* 'Aureum', the tufted hair grass (*Deschampsia cespitosa*) and the cord grass (*Spartina pectinata* 'Aureomarginata') also make subtle planting companions.

Top right
In a subtropical garden, fan and sword palms mix wih strelitzias, calla lilies and *Cyperus papyrus*.
Centre right
A fine *Aloe dichotoma* is in flower surrounded by spiky yuccas, echeverias and other aloes.
Right
These rigid-leaved *Phormium* 'Maori Sunrise', *P.* 'Guardsman' and *Yucca thompsoniana* retain their spiky form throughout the year.

Using Dome-Shaped Plants Many plant shapes are as useful as the garden's architectural surroundings, making positive, three-dimensional statements that are as strong as those made in stone or brick. It is possible to adapt nature by clipping compact shrubs like box, myrtle and yew into dense hedges. The natural form of many plants, however, can fulfil the same function and there are some plants whose naturally rounded form is an asset in the design of the garden. Many of them are inert, rounded evergreens, slow-growing and unresponsive to wind including cacti, hebes, santolina and lavenders.

Another useful, rounded shrub is *Viburnum davidii* whose ovate leaves are large, clearly delineated and inscribed with almost parallel veining unlike the dense texture of the tiny-leaved box, smaller hebes and myrtles. This dark, glossy evergreen is a foil for the more fragile leaves of plants like artemisia and its fairly stolid shape flatters formless shrubs such as weigela. You should also consider some of the smaller, naturally rounded conifers and the tiny, red and very rounded *Berberis thunbergii* 'Bagatelle'.

The slightly looser forms of some flowering shrubs such as *Potentilla fruticosa* varieties are also fairly static, rounded shapes. These very attractive plants enliven a shrub border for three to four months in summer with flowers varying from white through cream to yellow, orange and recently nearly red. The evergreen *Cistus* family have similar flowers, primrose-shaped but larger. Not all *Cistus* are able to cope with harsh climates but I find *C.* x *hybridus* (syn. *C.* x *corbariensis*), with its dark claret-coloured buds opening to pure white flowers, both reliable and charming. *C.* x *skanbergii* is slightly less frost-proof and has narrow, greyish foliage and delicate pink flowers. Just as appealing but with glossy, evergreen leaves is *Choisya ternata* and its sibling *C.* 'Aztec Pearl'. The former has a diameter of 2.5 m (8 ft) and the latter is slightly smaller. Both have aromatic leaves and fragrant, star-shaped, white flowers in spring and, if you are lucky, again in autumn.

Top left

Rounded, neatly clipped *Santolina pinnata neapolitana* 'Edward Bowles' creates formal edging for a gravel-lined border containing *Sidalcea* 'Rose Queen' and perennial *Artemisia lactiflora* with its dark green, toothed leaves.

Left

Dome-shaped plants, many of which are clipped into shape, have a strong influence on this garden. They include daisy-flowered *Erigeron karvinskianus*, *Ballota acetabulosa*, rosemary and santolina while the lime-green flowers of the *Euphorbia characias* are naturally spherical.

Strong architectural form is a valuable means of strengthening a design. If you are prepared to clip shapes, then you can have any form you wish. *Buxus microphylla* 'Green Pillow' is naturally rounded, as its name suggests, but all the box family can be clipped into geometric forms, even 'cloud shapes', as can the densely leaved evergreen loniceras. Do not forget the lavenders, such as *Lavandula angustifolia* 'Hidcote' or the cotton lavenders (*Santolina chamaecyparissus*). These can be clipped into formal mounds and massed together within parterres or used to edge rose or herb beds. Other shrubs give the impression of an overall dome-shaped habit. For example, the evergreen upright shrub *Euphorbia characias wulfenii* has dramatic spikes of large, ball-shaped, yellow-green flowers in the spring.

There are also some herbaceous perennials with a rounded form. They include daisy-flowered plants such as *Erigeron karvinskianus*, *Coreopsis verticillata* and *Anthemis punctata cupaniana*. Marguerites (*Argyranthemum frutescens*, syn. *Chrysanthemum frutescens*) have a finely leaved, mounded structure as do some geraniums although not all are tidy. Look for *Geranium renardii*, *G. sylvaticum* and *G. sanguineum* varieties. At a higher level the flower trusses of Joe Pye weed (*Eupatorium purpureum*) are mounded with a cumulus-cloud formation that echoes other spherical forms.

Some rounded forms are open to the sky, creating a more bowl-like profile. Dogwoods (*Cornus*) are well-loved in winter when their distinctive shape is most visible. Their coloured stems, ranging from bright green through to yellow and red bring much cheer in the cold season. If cut to ground level each spring their natural habit is to curve gently from the centre and reach up to attain their ultimate height. *C. stolonifera* 'Flaviramea' produces green and yellow shoots, *C. alba* and its varieties have rich red stems and all look very effective placed with *C. a.* 'Kesselringii' whose upright stems are a very dark purple. These dogwoods look better in the wilder garden associated with elder, wild roses, viburnums and willows.

Top right

Very static mounds of clipped santolina and erigeron in this garden have been maintained with the utmost precision; they are nevertheless just as decorative when they are in flower. The pink and white, daisy-like flowers of the *Erigeron karvinskianus* appear in the summer and autumn.

Right

The upright form of this tall *Trichocereus pasacana* grows among a sea of the sculptural *Echinocactus grusonii* to create an animated scene. Here they are enhanced by the modelling effect of the bright sunlight.

A Ball-Themed Garden This elegantly simple plot is part of a large, richly planted, northern California garden in which a small, quiet corner has been designed with a repetition of domed shapes. The owner described the garden as 'crafted' and the design shows a clear, aesthetic eye. The overall design is dependent on repeated forms and architectural plants for its effect. It is an intimate space, planted with thoughtful care so that all the chosen plants are in perfect proportion.

The ball shapes mostly come from different varieties of santolina. They include mossily green *Santolina rosmarinifolia rosmarinifolia* (syn. *S. viridis*), *S. pinnata* and silver-leaved *S. chamaecyparissus* 'Lemon Queen'. In the foreground, *Convolvulus cneorum* is also neatly maintained as a mound as are the lavenders. These have been chosen for their dense habit and include thickly foliaged English lavender (*Lavandula angustifolia* 'Hidcote') and *L. stoechas* 'Otto Quast'.

The natural habit of *Erigeron karvinskianus* is less disciplined than the santolinas and lavenders but it also mounds naturally and softens the overall formality. *Ballota acetabulosa* has the same effect but should be trimmed after flowering. The tidy *Echinops ritro* 'Veitch's Blue' has very compact foliage but with tall flowers while the rosemary (*Rosmarinus officinalis* 'Tuscan Blue') duplicates this upwardly growing shape. *Euphorbia characias wulfenii* also makes a naturally rounded shape with similarly upright and rounded flower heads.

Texture is also an important aspect of the theme. The mossy santolinas, the woolly softness of the grey ballota and the catmint (*Nepeta*) as well as the sandstone ball all absorb light. Only the satin gleam of the *Convolvulus cneorum* reflects the light so that nothing distracts from the form. The ground between the paving stones is carpeted with velvety *Thymus serpyllum* 'Minimus' into which wild oxalis creep in, only to be weeded out.

First planting, below Originally a bog, the ground in this garden was raised by approximately 30 cm (1 ft) and drainage ditches were dug to draw off the excess water. Soil containing a mixture of turkey manure and woodchip dressing was then added. The resulting garden is therefore rather dry, conditions that are ideal for the Mediterranean plants that grow there.

First Planting

KEY *(H = Height; S = Spread)*

1. *Ballota acetabulosa,* *H and S: 60 cm (2 ft)*

2. *Lavandula angustifolia* 'Hidcote', *H and S: 75 cm (2½ ft)*

3. *Convolvulus cneorum,* *H and S: 75 cm (2½ ft)*

4. *Lotus hirsutus,* *H and S: 60 cm (2 ft)*

5. *Prunus lusitanica,* *H and S: 6-10 m (20-30 ft)*

6. *Erigeron karvinskianus,* *H: 10-15 cm (4-6 in)*

7. *Lavandula stoechas* 'Otto Quast', *H and S: 60 cm (2 ft)*

8. *Nepeta racemosa,* *H and S: 60 cm (2 ft)*

9. *Pittosporum tenuifolium,* *H: 6 m (20 ft); S: 3 m (10 ft)*

10. *Echinops ritro* 'Veitch's Blue', *H: 1.2 m (4 ft); S: 75 cm (2½ ft)*

11. *Euphorbia characias wulfenii,* *H and S: 1.2 m (4 ft)*

12. *Rosmarinus officinalis* 'Tuscan Blue', *H and S: 1.8 m (6 ft)*

13. *Thymus serpyllum* 'Minimus', *H: 5 cm (2 in)*

14. *Santolina pinnata,* *H: 75 cm (2½ ft); S: 90 cm (3 ft)*

15. *Santolina rosmarinifolia rosmarinifolia,* *H: 60 cm (2 ft); S: 90 cm (3 ft)*

16. *Santolina chamaecyparissus* 'Lemon Queen', *H: 75cm (2½ ft); S: 90 cm (3 ft)*

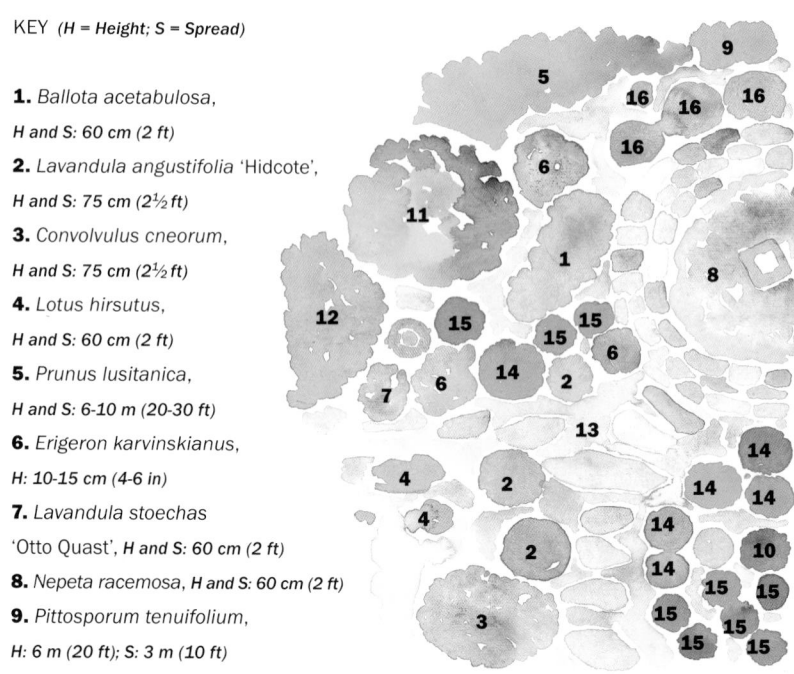

The colour scheme of the garden is very restrained with a mixture of green and silver-grey foliage combined with low-key flower hues. These are comprised of pastels and blues including the hazy blue flowers of grey-leaved catmint and work beautifully with the cool yellows and creams of the santolina flowers. The strongest colours come from lime-green euphorbia and the purple lavender.

The garden has avoided any temptations of froth, both in terms of the colours and the shapes of the plants. It retains a sense of scale and dimension because all the ball-shaped plants are kept neatly clipped. The enclosing fences also provide protection against the raging gales that attack the peninsula on which the garden is situated but it is the design that achieves a sense of static calm.

Second summer, right This overhead view of the finished garden shows clearly how the rounded theme of the garden has been developed. Every attention has been paid to detail. Although they are naturally squat the santolinas have been clipped in order to maintain their firm, rounded form and repeated throughout the garden to create striking, rhythmical patterns. The habit of the santolinas is emphasized not only by the presence of other dome-shaped plants but also by the sedentary spherical stone, the meandering path of circular paving slabs and the rounded terracotta pot.

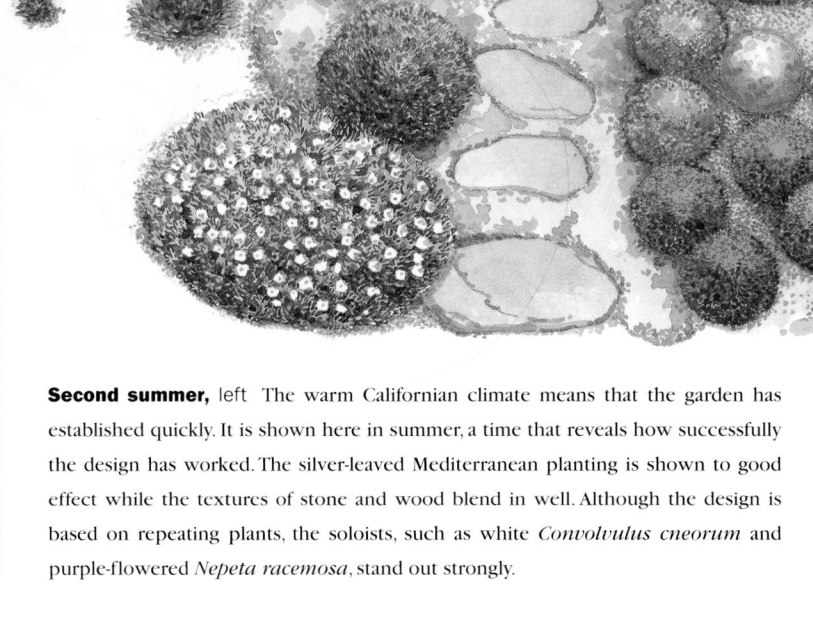

Second summer, left The warm Californian climate means that the garden has established quickly. It is shown here in summer, a time that reveals how successfully the design has worked. The silver-leaved Mediterranean planting is shown to good effect while the textures of stone and wood blend in well. Although the design is based on repeating plants, the soloists, such as white *Convolvulus cneorum* and purple-flowered *Nepeta racemosa*, stand out strongly.

TEXTURE AND PATTERN

Establishing the shapes in a garden is one thing but textures and patterns also need consideration. Plants have as much texture as fabrics: they can be rough, woolly or felted while others have a satin-like sheen or are as smooth as kid gloves. On the whole we respond to texture in a sensual way although it can also be experienced visually.

Pattern is not quite the same. It is about order and rhythm, whether this is a man-made, mathematical progression of lines, rectangles and circles or the random repeats found in nature such as the twinning of pinnate leaves on ash trees or the concentric circles of pompon dahlias. Here the value is decorative rather than sensual with the patterns created by plants being used to 'fill in' areas for purely ornamental reasons rather like wallpaper.

Left

Rust-red *Iris* 'Kent Pride' with erysimums, aquilegias, geraniums, heucheras and bronze fennel enhance the warm colours of this border.

Above

This border is prettily awash with a variety of textural details including massed grasses, finely haired seed-heads and velvet-like sedum flowers.

AN INTRODUCTION TO TEXTURE

The textures to which we all respond are those that we stroke. As children we are all attracted by the emotive power of tactile textures. We trail our fingers through grasses; idly pluck the leaves from *Stachys byzantina*, even putting it to the face to reap the full furry benefit; break open the cases of sweet chestnuts to feel the velvet inside; and regard the pussy willow as compulsory to the touch in spring. This physical appreciation rolls over into adult life, making many ornamental plants both appealing and desirable. A mass of the same plant would be predictable and boring. So it is necessary to draw attention to these tactile plants by siting them with more neutral ones such as geraniums, filipendulas or heucheras.

Mirroring life, not all textures are comfortable, cosy and inviting. Some are crisp and precise, others are dramatically spiked and some warn us to stand clear. Such tensions are the stuff of life. Blandness is not exciting nor does it spur the creative forces and so juxtaposing dissimilar surfaces creates dialogue in the garden. The plainer leaf, undemanding but reassuring, is the leitmotif of plant association, the genial background support to other more competitive relationships such as prickly eryngiums combined with soft lady's mantle (*Alchemilla mollis*).

The texture of foliage and flowers can also have a very influential effect upon the power of colour and on how we perceive colour. Colour is of course highly emotive, either inviting or austere, cool or warm. Indeed, every woman knows that velvet or satin fabrics have an enriching effect on colour and that the identical dye will never look as intense if used on cotton, even to the same level of saturation. According to this principle, the velvet-like foliage of the conifer *Chamaecyparis obtusa* looks rich green compared with the more average green of the open-textured Leyland cypress (X *Cupressocyparis leylandii*). Similarly, the intense colour of the very popular but rather tender perennial chocolate *Cosmos atrosanguineus* lies in the velvet-rich texture of its dark red flower petals.

The glaucous hostas, on the other hand, are not warmly endearing. Their cool 'Wedgwood blue', caused by a waxy coating on the leaves, distances them, making for a chill, architectural quality. This effect is also evident in the common name of *Sedum spectabile* 'Iceberg', the ice-plant, whose hard fleshy texture produces a rigid, jade-green foliage. S. 'Herbstfreude' is an example of a plant where two opposing textures create contrary effects on colour. The hard, smooth, fleshy leaves have a pastel-pale clarity whereas

Top right
Hazy love-in-a-mist (*Nigella damascena*) flowers are grown here with velvet *Stachys byzantina*.
Centre right
This mop-head hydrangea looks solid next to the soft, fluffy flowers of *Astilbe* 'Ostrich Plume'.
Right
***Phlomis tuberosa* 'Amazone' has whorls of lilac-pink flowers that contrast with the sharp, silvery leaves of an *Onopordum acanthium*.**

Top right
Bronze fennel (*Foeniculum vulgare* 'Purpureum') creates an insubstantial haze among these neat, drumstick-like flowers of *Allium hollandicum*.
Right
These herbaceous plants, including many with small flowers such as *Knautia macedonica*, astrantias, campanulas, violas and phlox, have a tapestry-like effect and are combined with spiny eryngiums, shasta daisies and veronicastrums.

the flattened, massed flower heads, which turn from intense pink to opulent bronze as the season ends, appear velvety. In such a way, texture has a direct influence upon the senses.

However, the most exciting point about texture is not the trickery but the beauties of contrast that it creates and the sensual responses it provokes throughout the garden. The distinctly different textures of plants that enjoy full sun and the contrasts between them can be very pleasing.

For example, the gritty leaves of crassulas, hairy dorycniums, silken *Convolvulus cneorum* and the sparse foliage of branching teucriums are just a few very compatible friends. In damp shade, leaves tend to be larger and the textures are likely to be different. You might also like to contrast the huge, hairy, heart-shaped leaves of *Trachystemon orientalis*, which cover large areas, with taller, ferny-leaved plants such as *Astilbe* 'Professor van der Wielen'.

TEXTURAL COMBINATIONS

The following pages will look in more detail at the main tactile textures – coarse, prickly, smooth and woolly – and also at those plants whose textural impact is largely visual. How you combine these textures depends very much upon whether you want to use texture decoratively or to foster a certain atmosphere, mysterious or romantic.

Using Coarse-Leaved Plants Garden plants are not all the 'delicate flowers' of poetic fantasy. Many have to protect themselves against the vagaries of nature. The surface of the leaves can fulfil a number of functions, whether to deflect intense sunlight or to slow down the rate of evaporation in exposed windy sites. Lamiums protect themselves by imitating stinging nettles while members of the borage family have a chin-bristle leaf surface to protect them from slugs. Such strongly textured leaves are invaluable in the garden where contrast adds piquancy. After all, a smooth soft cheese is a joy accompanied by a hard crisp apple. Rough surfaces also absorb light and so create a stillness in the garden.

One of the roughest foliage surfaces belongs to *Gunnera manicata* whose puckered leaves contrast with the surface of water. If this plant is too large for your garden try the moisture-loving ornamental rhubarb (*Rheum palmatum*) whose leaves have deep incisions. It could be grown beside the rather elegant ostrich fern (*Matteuccia struthiopteris*). Rheums also have tall flower spikes which, combined with their foliage, might provide an attractive contrast to the fluffy flowers of *Thalictrum aquilegiifolium* in early summer.

The coarsely textured leaves of *Rodgersia podophylla* would be an excellent neighbour for this group. It has bronzed, grainy, leathery leaves, which are heavily incut and sculptural, and looks distinctive among plants that like damp soil. It contrasts with the immaculately tidy hostas but is also effectively flattered by a close association with the large *Astilbe rivularis* or the equally coppered *A.* 'Superba'. All the astilbes have richly textured foliage that makes them highly versatile companions for different plants.

On the whole shrubs have smooth leaves but those of *Viburnum rhytidophyllum* have an exceptionally rough surface. Not everyone is a fan of this tall evergreen, which can reach over 3 m (10 ft) tall, but it appeals to me. The long, narrow leaves hang down, showing deeply corrugated veining. Their undersides flip over in the wind to reveal the parchment-coloured felting that covers the stems. Clearly, although these coarse-textured plants are not to everyone's liking, I look upon them as a means of providing a contrast to more delicate companions. *Vive la différence.*

Far left
An ostrich fern (*Matteuccia struthiopteris*) thrives with rhododendrons, azaleas, hostas and primulas.

Top left
Huge leaves of *Gunnera manicata* are coarsely puckered and have a jagged outline.

Left
Rodgersia podophylla, R. pinnata and hostas all have neatly shaped leaves that create patterns.

Top right
Richly textured *Heuchera* 'Palace Purple' foliage flatters the red flowers of helianthemum.

Centre right
Aegopodium podagraria 'Variegatum', Alchemilla mollis and anchusa create rich foliage textures.

Right
Pink saxifrage flowers, lime euphorbia and a variegated lamium create a detailed textural effect.

Using Prickly Plants There are many prickly plants to choose from that are for looking at rather than for touching. They serve a highly provocative role, bringing drama to the garden. Some of these are so prickly that they can be dangerous and should not be used where children may play. These include the rock-hard, spiny agaves, members of the prickly sea holly family (*Eryngium*) and the piercing swords of yuccas including Spanish dagger (*Yucca gloriosa*) with its stiff, spiny, grey-green leaves and *Y. gloriosa* 'Variegata' with its

---

PRICKLY PLANTS

Acanthus spinosus (Bear's Breeches)
A 1.2 m (4 ft) perennial with large, dark green, deeply divided basal leaves. The flower spires are mauve and resemble foxgloves. It will tolerate lightly shaded conditions.

Echinops bannaticus 'Taplow Blue' (Globe Thistle)
A 2.2 m (7 ft) tall sun-loving perennial with drumstick-shaped stems, prickly foliage and metallic blue flowers.

---

the compact, blue-flowered *Echinops ritro* and the taller, paler blue *E. bannaticus* 'Taplow Blue' will grow companionably in the same environment. The spiny eryngiums, from the rapier-like *Eryngium agavifolium* to the far less dangerous but equally attractive *E. bourgatii*, add dramatic texture to the garden, particularly when grown with soft, pretty foliage such as geraniums or *Alchemilla mollis*. *E.* 'Miss Willmott's Ghost' is a metallic colour while *E. variifolium* is blueish and this earns them a position among the

Above left
Agave americana has sword-shaped, prickly leaves that look static and sculptural.
Above right
Dark green, spiny cacti contrast dramatically with the more delicate silvery leaves of these aloes.

Eryngium bourgatii (Sea Holly)
All sea hollies will thrive in hot, sunny sites that have good drainge. This silver-foliaged perennial grows to a height of 60 cm (2 ft). The stems are tinged with blue and carry attractive, teasel-like flowers.

Mahonia aquifolium (Oregon Grape)
A 1.2 m (4 ft) tall evergreen shrub that has reddish foliage and clusters of blue fruit in the autumn. It has glossy, spiny leaves and fragrant, yellow flowers in the spring. It will also provide an excellent ground cover in the shade.

Above left
This rigidly spiky agave sits among the blueish, fleshy, spiny rosettes of X *Pachyveria glauca*.
Above right
One of the prettiest of the prickly plants, *Eryngium* x *oliverianum* is seen here with variegated comfrey.

---

sword-shaped leaves. There are also some 'would-be' spiky plants such as cardoons that look sharp but are not unforgiving should anyone fall into them. They fall into that group of plants that have textural value because of their visual impact (see pages 54-57).

The genuinely prickly plants are usually able to cope with dryish conditions. So globe thistles such as

summer flowers in a traditional herbaceous border. If you have a hot, free-draining and gravelled site, also include the biennial Blessed Mary's thistle (*Silybum marianum*) with its marbled leaves and prickly flower heads. This has marbled rosettes in the first year and thistle-like flowers in the second, giving you an unpredictable succession of effects every year.

Less threatening, but distinctly prickly, the seed-heads of wild teasels, which are members of the *Dipsacus* family, add a thistle-like contrast to other wild biennial associates such as frilly petalled cornflowers (*Centaurea*) and tissue-paper poppies (*Papaver*). They can also be successfully linked with perennial ornamental grasses such as the furry *Pennisetum orientale* or the oat-like inflorescences of *Stipa calamagrostis*. The huge spiny Scotch thistle (*Onopordum acanthium*) has the same biennial seed

PRICKLY PLANTS

***Olearia* x *macrodonta* (Daisy Bush)**
An evergreen holly-like shrub that grows to 2.5 m (8 ft) with clusters of white flowers and gold, patterned foliage. Prefers well-drained soil that does not dry out.

***Onorpordum acanthium*
(Scotch Thistle)**
This silver biennial, with spiny leaves and pink flowers, grows to 1.8 m (6 ft) and needs sun and free-draining soil.

All these plants can also be echoed in the garden scheme by other prickly grasses and shrubs. If you want shrubs with real prickles then the leaves of certain forms of mahonia and berberis are positively hostile. *Berberis julianae*, for example, is an evergreen shrub with scented yellow flowers and is one of the tallest and most spiny of the berberis family. Many of the mahonias are also scented and *Mahonia* x *media* 'Winter Sun' is worth considering. Both the berberis and the mahonia do well in light or shady

Above left
This *Cynara cardunculus* with its green-grey, jagged foliage has terminal, purple, thistle flower heads.
Above right
These striking, succulent aloes are set off perfectly by the massed yellow flowers of crassula.

Osmanthus heterophyllus
This shrub, which grows to a height of 2.5 m (8 ft), is holly-like in appearance with grey leaves and white daisy flowers. The leaves, although prickly, are white-felted underneath.

***Silybum marianum*
(Blessed Mary's Thistle)**
A biennial that has attractive, white-marbled rosettes of prickly leaves above which pink flowers grow to a height of 1.2 m (4 ft) in the next summer. This thistle can also thrive in any garden soil.

Above left
Purple lavender (*Lavandula stoechas*) grows among a mass of finely prickly eryngiums.
Above right
The thin, succulent leaves of this red-tinged *Dyckia* are edged with fierce-looking spines.

distribution but it is a dramatic and dangerous soloist. Alternatively, in really hot, dry conditions, the spikily charming alpine thistle (*Carlina acaulis*) planted at ground level is a much more suitable choice. These plants should be contrasted with the velvety, sage-green herb *Marrubium vulgare* or with the silken sheen of *Convolvulus cneorum*.

conditions. This means that they can be successfully flattered by a froth of ferns or contrasted with a collar of massed *Hemerocallis* 'Stella de Oro'. Other prickly mahonias include the Oregon grape (*Mahonia aquifolium*) with its glossy but prickly evergreen leaves and *M.* x *media* 'Buckland'. This mahonia has toothed leaves and yellow flower spikes.

Using Smooth-Leaved Plants The value of plants with smooth, shiny leaves is to reflect light back into other spaces. In deeply shaded areas this has obvious benefits both on plants and on their visual impact. A polished evergreen such as cherry laurel (*Prunus laurocerasus*) is a popular example. Other forms such as *P. l.* 'Otto Luyken' have glossy, dark green leaves and white flower spikes in late spring .

Equally suited to shade is the burnished evergreen *Fatsia japonica* whose shiny leaves bring light into dark areas. All of these plants can be flattered by the contrasting texture of *Dryopteris* and *Polystichum* ferns throughout the year and by spring bulbs. They can also be lightened by the arching foliage of the false spikenard (*Smilacina racemosa*) or encouraged by fluffy tiarella flowers and anemone hybrids such as pale pink *Anemone hupehensis* 'September Charm' or the autumn-flowering, white *A.* x *hybrida* 'Luise Uhink'.

Bountifully flowered rhododendrons with smooth, glossy foliage will succeed in acidic soils and light shade. Here too astilbes and ferns will provide a striking contrast. The smooth-leaved, glossy *Asplenium* ferns planted in the mass as well as other ground covers such as the gleaming round leaves of *Asarum europaeum* or polished *Pachyphragma macrophyllum* also blend in. If larger reflective leaves are required consider the many species of hellebore, such as long-lasting Corsican hellebore (*Helleborus argutifolius*) and *H. orientalis*. North American plants such as

Maianthemum bifolium and *Cornus canadensis* also thrive in acidic soils while the pretty evergreen *Pachysandra* covers the ground just as well.

Bergenias may be known as the poor man's hosta but these tough plants will grow in shade or sun and have lustrous, overlapping, rounded leaves in a range of different colours from greens to red-purples. *Bergenia* 'Ballawley' has shiny, evergreen leaves that turn red in the winter while *B. crassifolia* turns a mahogany colour. They make a positive reflective statement either as a ground-cover or as lush edging. *Arum italicum* and some *Ligularia* operate at a higher level but have the same glossy attraction. *L. dentata* 'Desdemona' is more appreciated for its purpled, glossy leaves than for its shaggy yellow flowers.

It is not just the glossy evergreens that have this gloriously shiny effect. Grasses such as *Miscanthus sinensis* also catch the light. Many have a sheen to their leaves while those that are naturally curved show this off to still greater effect. Glossy sun-loving plants are less numerous but there are a few to choose from including the apple-green griselinia, the shiny aeoniums and the pittosporums, a genus of evergreen trees and shrubs. The evergreen crispness of these shrubs is an asset among flowering shrubs once they have finished flowering, fitting in well in a mixed border. Let the herbaceous flowers have their fifteen minutes of fame while foliage plants provide the mainstay of the display.

Top near right
A run of overlapping, glossy, evergreen bergenia leaves fringe *Hamamelis* x *intermedia* in the autumn.
Centre near right
Arum italicum 'Pictum' has beautiful, arrow-shaped, marbled foliage which is decorative in winter.
Bottom near right
In a subtropical garden *Hippeastrum*, a member of the amaryllis family, flowers above smooth, narrow leaves.

Centre Top
Smooth leaves are characteristic of these cannas and the banana *Musa basjoo*.
Top far right
Groups of green and black aeoniums create decorative patterns behind this striking phormium.
Bottom far right
Blue-flowered *Vinca minor* 'Argenteovariegata' trails amid lime-green euphorbia, ferns and acaenas.

Using Woolly Plants In the midst of the flowers and leaves of the garden, it is the woolly, often grey, leaves that always stand out, their silvery hairs catching the light and inviting us to touch them. They are ideal for displaying other plant textures and patterns but they are also individualists. Probably the plant most easily named by those who declare they know nothing about plants is *Stachys byzantina*, commonly known as

possible. Wool-covered leaves protect the plant from the heat but they also reduce the efficient manufacture of chlorophyll and so maximum exposure to light is essential. Many woolly leaved plants thus come from Mediterranean climates although even these efficient plants also need to conserve moisture. Sages favour dry, sunny sites and have interesting textures. For example, the leaves of the annual or biennial painted sage

(*Salvia viridis*) have a soft downy surface while the flowers have flamboyant, purple bracts that appear in the summer.

Planting in gravel reduces evaporation and is therefore popular with many gardeners. This setting also enhances the appearance of woolly plants because the gritty texture of the gravel is a perfect foil for their softness. For this reason those plants that are stone-hard like sedums,

bunnies' ears or lamb's tongues. Other woolly leaved plants include the hirsute dorycniums, the velvet-leaved *Hydrangea aspera* Villosa Group and Jerusalem sage (*Phlomis fruticosa*). They will all act as moderators among spiky or hard-edged shrubs and herbaceous plants or will lighten a rather serious mass of evergreens.

With very few exceptions plants with grey and hairy foliage need the benefit of as much sun as

Above left
Few leaves are as woolly as those of *Verbascum bombyciferum*, which is seen here in contrast with smooth-leaved *Sedum telephium*.
Above centre
***Stachys byzantina* is a very woolly leaved plant and is grown here interwoven with blue veronica.**
Above right
Flowers can be surprisingly woolly as can be seen from the trailing, red flowers of this love-lies-bleeding (*Amaranthus caudatus*).

houseleeks (*Sempervivum*) and echeverias make contrasting companions for the woolly thyme (*Thymus pseudolanuginosus*) or perhaps the California native *Eriophyllum lanatum*, a spreading plant with yellow flowers over white, woolly foliage cushions. With these plants, the rounded, sage-grey leaves of *Geranium renardii* also provide a subtle relationship as they are slightly soft and downy. You might also like to consider the finely feathered *Tanacetum densum amani* with its velvet-like appearance. To complete the picture, you could add some clumps of *Hieracium villosum*, a hawkweed that has yellow dandelion-like flowers that rise 30 cm (1 ft) above the matted, hairy, grey-green leaves.

In an herbaceous mix, the tender *Lavandula lanata* is a small shrub that can be used to define the mayhem of summer. Its very woolly, bushy

This might be added as well as some tall agapanthus and perhaps some *Campanula persicifolia* nearby to share the fun.

The biennial *Verbascum bombyciferum* has perhaps the woolliest leaves of all. Its character is quite different during its two years of life as the white rosette of thickly woolly leaves stretch out to support a tall 1.8 m (6 ft) spire that is still woolly but carries citrus-yellow flowers. The variety

V. b. 'Silver Lining' may take three years to perform but during this time the diameter of the rosettes increase. This plant will reproduce itself by seeding easily throughout gravel gardens. It is a fine co-habiter with the equally grey and tall Californian tree poppy (*Romneya coulteri*) which has rather crumpled, tissue-like, white flowers and jagged foliage. Another interesting companion for this group is the perennial *Verbena bonariensis*

foliage is pure white, which is in dramatic contrast with its dark blue flowers. Place it near some groups of tidy blue *Salvia nemorosa* 'East Friesland', in association with meandering, silvery *Stachys byzantina* 'Silver Carpet' and include some drifts of cream-flowered achilleas. All these plants are suited to well-drained soils as is the short-lived, 80 cm (32 in) tall *Salvia argentea* with its woolly white leaves and white, hooded flowers.

Above left
Phlomis fruticosa and ***Salvia officinalis***
Purpurascens Group have velvety leaves while those of *Macleaya cordata* are smooth as leather.
Above centre
Delicately coloured leaves of *Salvia officinalis* 'Tricolor' are particularly soft to the touch.
Above right
The velvety leaves of *Sedum spectabile* blend with the equally soft *Stachys byzantina* and contrast with the smooth leaves of *Bergenia* 'Morning Red'.

which has a tall, branching habit. When grown in groups, this plant has many small, tuft-like, claret-coloured flowers that would not clash with the yellow verbascum particularly if a number of *Stachys byzantina* 'Primrose Heron' were massed together to act as woolly linking agents. Alternatively, the ferny foliage and lemon-yellow flowers of *Centaurea ruthenica* would also make a suitably sympathetic friend.

Using Visual Textures Many textures are more important visually than they are from a tactile point of view. For example, there are 'would-be' spiked plants including phormiums and irises, architectural acanthus and the magnificent cardoon (*Cynara cardunculus*) that only look sharp or prickly to the touch. They serve an important role in the garden, providing a clear, spiky focus in the froth of summer simply because they are so clearly sculptural and linear.

In contrast, many plants have an insubstantial shape that brings an airy grace and an indefinable charm to the overall picture in the garden. Using an image of fragility to emphasize another's strength is a method commonly used in Hollywood and it is equally applicable in the garden. The lacy artemisias, the frondy ferns such as *Polystichum aculeatum* and *Dryopteris affinis* Crispa Group and the hazy flowers of baby's breath (*Gypsophila*), for example, will lighten the more serious plants like yuccas and eryngiums.

Among the foliage plants artemisias are especially valued for their fine, linear tracery. They revel in dry, sunny conditions and are invaluable

planting partners for such sculptural plants as stiff *Euphorbia characias*, spiky *Salvia nemorosa* and statuesque *Acanthus spinosus* or *A. mollis*. The silvery white foliage of *Artemisia arborescens* 'Faith Raven', for example, massed among heavy mounds of white-flowered cistus or *Carpenteria californica*, looks all the more fragile in contrast. In fact, when you use closely allied colours, it is often only the contrast of textures that distinguishes one plant from another. This is effectively shown when the almost white, lacy foliage of *A. alba* 'Canescens' is closely associated with the silvery-green sheen of *Convolvulus cneorum*.

The herb fennel (*Foeniculum vulgare*) with its delicate, filigree-like foliage also has a strong visual impact on a garden border. Subtle relationships can be created using bronze fennel (*Foeniculum vulgare* 'Purpureum') as a backing for the strikingly coloured *Helenium* 'Copper Spray' or perhaps green fennel beside *Phygelius aequalis* 'Yellow Trumpet'. Culinary fennel also complements simple flower shapes and is often used in association with herbaceous perennials in order to provide an insubstantial textural back-

Top left
Pale purple flowers of *Perovskia atriplicifolia* have a hazy texture that contrasts with the smooth flowers of *Lavatera assurgentiflora* 'Barnsley'.

Centre left
Apricot-coloured, velvety flower heads of achillea blend in with the fluffy seed-heads of clematis.

Left
Coarse, green-and-white variegated leaves of deadnettle (*Lamium maculatum* 'Beacon Silver') contrast very well with the more lacy, filigree-like textures of *Artemisia* 'Powis Castle' and *A. ludoviciana* 'Valerie Finnis'. These plants also associate well through their silvery colour which emphasizes their textural differences.

Right
Shown in high summer, this green-coloured border depends largely on the textural impact of different types of foliage for its overall effect. The visual texture is dominated by the delicate haze of tall green fennel (*Foeniculum vulgare*). The indistinct effect of these feather-like plants provides the perfect background for the other more sturdy plants in the border. These plants include the yellow vertical spires of lupins as well as the golden yellow foliage of oregano that has been planted at regular intervals along the length of the border. These herbs spill out over the gravel pathway, which has the effect of softening the border edge and creating a repeating pattern.

ground to their rather more defined patterns. Similarly, in a sunny site, the apple-green, whispery-fine leaves of *Asparagus officinalis* can be flattered at foot by its kitchen companion, the touchingly velvet-leaved grey sage (*Salvia officinalis*). The fast-growing annual *Nigella damascena*, which is commonly known as love-in-a-mist, has blue or white flowers and looks particularly attractive when combined with purple sage (*S. officinalis* Purpurascens Group). It associates both texturally through its very fine, feathery leaves and later in the year because of the colour of its striped, purple-red seed-heads.

In hot, dry countries, the needle-fine leaves of plants such as the tamarisk (*Tamarix ramoissima*, syn. *T. pentandra*) prevent water loss and make the overall texture of the tree look hazy and insubstantial. As a result, there is a natural sympathy if it is grown in combination with Mediterranean plants including rock roses (*Helianthemum*), lavender, santolina and rosemary at foot or in dramatic contrast with the powerful shapes of agaves, cordylines or yuccas. In fact, any plant that has the word 'laciniata' in its name will have narrowly slashed leaves. For example, *Sambucus nigra laciniata* and *Rhus glabra* 'Laciniata' both have finely feathered foliage that looks particularly effective

Top far left
This white garden scheme is dependent on a variety of textures and patterns. The tiny flowers of *Crambe cordifolia* are massed behind *Campanula persicifolia alba* accompanied by the feathery grass *Sorghastrum avenaceum* and *Viola cornuta* Alba Group.

Top near left
The host of feathery textures in this bed comes from *Alchemilla mollis* and pink astilbes.

Left
This flowing garden scheme contains *Monarda* in association with *Persicaria amplexicaulis*, both of which have a very distinctive form compared with the hazy flowers of *Helictotrichon sempervirens*.

PLANTS WITH VISUAL TEXTURES

Adiantum venustum
A finely fronded deciduous fern with light green, delicate foliage in spring. It grows to 23 cm (9 in) tall with a spread of 30 cm (12 in) and prefers a damp, semi-shaded site with acidic soil.

***Gypsophila paniculata* 'Bristol Fairy'**
A hardy perennial with fine, wiry, branching stems that support a cloud of tiny, white flowers in the summer. It grows up to 75 cm (2½ ft) tall with a spread of 45 cm (1½ ft) and prefers a sunny site with well-drained soil.

***Pinus strobus* 'Radiata'**
A small, slow-growing pine covered with very fine, silver-blue needles from which young shoots emerge in the spring. It may reach up to 1.2 m (4 ft) tall but grow over 1.5 m (5 ft) wide.

***Saxifraga fortunei* 'Rubrifolia'**
This low-growing perennial is suited to mass planting and supports airy sprays of white flowers that contrast with the neat rosettes of reddish-coloured leaves. It prefers a sheltered, shaded site with moist soil and has a height and spread of 30 cm (12 in).

***Stipa gigantea* (Golden Oats)**
A perennial grass with narrow leaves and fine, oat-like flower panicles in summer that are silvery or bronze depending on the light. It grows to 2.5 m (8 ft) tall and 90 cm (3 ft) wide.

Thalictrum aquilegiifolium album
This is a white form of the usually lilac-coloured hardy perennial which has attractive, finely divided, greyish foliage and attractive, fluffy flowers. It requires sun or light shade and well-drained soil. It grows to a height of 1.2m (4 ft) tall and has a spread of 45 cm (1½ ft).

---

among the more sculptural leaves of many species of evergreen viburnum or prunus. In just the same way, feathery ferns provide a marvellous foil for hellebores and hostas because they all enjoy growing in damp shady conditions. Indeed textural combinations always will succeed when you combine plants that originate from a similar habitat even if this is from different places across the globe (see 'Natural Compatibility', on pages 112-31).

Visual textures are not exclusive to foliage. There is also a variety of flowers including spiraeas, shade-tolerant astilbes and aruncus that have a feathery texture. These feathery flowers flatter the leather-heavy leaves of bergenias or the layered graphic perfection of the larger hostas. Herbaceous flowers can also be as light as thistledown. Gypsophila, thalictrum, catmint (*Nepeta*) and perovskia all have particularly hazy flowers and can be used in sun-filled areas to provide a welcome relief and add an air of frivolity to borders that are awash with vibrant pattern and clamouring shapes.

The flowers of the rather aptly named smoke tree (*Cotinus coggygria*) are cloud-like, adding a different dimension to fairly substantial shrubs such as the New Zealand daisy bush (*Olearia* x *macrodonta*) with its greyish, felted leaves. The spring- to autumn-flowering gypsophila is perhaps the most ethereal of all these flowers with names such as 'Rosy Veil' and 'Bristol Fairy' clearly indicating its nature.

From late spring to early summer heucheras hold tiny flowers in suspension at the border edge. In mid-summer catmint is covered with fine sprays of pale blue flowers while later on in the year *Calamintha nepeta glandulosa* 'White Cloud' has a profusion of tiny flowers above ground. Towards the end of the season Russian sage (*Perovskia* 'Blue Spire') can provide a hazy contrast to forms of *Phlox paniculata*.

CREATING PLANT PATTERNS

Patterns exist in the garden whether we planned them or not. The eye picks out decorative rhythms when plants with the same form imitate each other from one area of the garden to another. As we will see, pattern can also exist by echoing the same leaf or flower shape all over the garden, by using plants with distinctive foliage or by including plants with a dramatic outline to their leaves.

However, there is a more random way in which the eye perceives pattern and this is by unconsciously sorting out shapes and linking them through suggestion. Instantly visible columnar plants are a case in point with spires of burning bush (*Dictamnus*) linking with gay feather (*Liatris spicata*), a slightly more furry upright and elsewhere with the bristly pokers of kniphofia. Similarly, a mass of *Veronicastrum virginicum* or

V. v. album will be in tension with a mass of *Salvia nemorosa* 'East Friesland'. These rhythms also occur with grass-like forms. Thus, irises link with sisyrinchiums, phormiums link with yuccas, miscanthus echoes pampas grass and rhythmical patterns are created. Links between strong leaf shapes can also be forged with the dramatic, incised, grey foliage of *Cynara cardunculus* echoing silver-grey artemisias.

The Rhythm of Repeats There are two ways of achieving decorative rhythms. The first method is traditionally formal and uses geometric, often symmetrical, grid patterns. Identical plants may be an equal distance apart or beds might be outlined with a hedge to create geometric harmony. Those who are seeking geometric, mathematical precision could plant iberis, daisies or zinnias arranged in circular patterns and edged by grey-leaved *Artemisia stelleriana*.

Above left
Rosa 'Iceberg', planted at intervals with silver *Cynara cardunculus*, creates a repeat pattern.
Above right
The thin leaves of this *Carex* grass echo the stately form of a *Phormium* 'Sundowner'.
Top far right
Bands of feverfew, *Santolina pinnata neapolitana* and *Anthemis tinctoria* 'E. C. Buxton' look dotty.
Far right
This bed contains repeating spikes of *Verbascum chaixii*, ligularias, lupins and delphiniums.

Flowers perform in much the same way. For example, annual hollyhocks (*Alcea rosea*) link with biennial verbascums while the fluffy flowers of goat's beard (*Aruncus dioicus*) can be mirrored elsewhere by white *Astilbe* 'Snowdrift' or *A.* 'White Gloria'. The globe thistle, *Echinops bannaticus* 'Taplow Blue', with its rounded, deep blue flower heads will stand out in a flummery of summer flowers and link with the huge *Allium giganteum* or the smaller *A. hollandicum* 'Purple Sensation'

with the same drumstick form. In damper areas, the drumstick primulas (*Primula denticulata*) with rounded, pale lavender flowers in spring can be echoed by the flowers of candelabra primulas held in parallel whorls. Planted among damp-loving ferns these rhythms are utterly charming.

Smaller flowers are very effective for creating patterns. Daisy-flowered plants such as coreopsis, rudbeckias and chrysanthemums can echo the same flower shape all over the garden while some herbaceous plants have a mass of flowers that create a richly decorative, dotty pattern. These include the lemon-yellow, button-like flowers of *Santolina rosmarinifolia rosmarinifolia* and the white flowers of *Achillea ptarmica* 'The Pearl'. From a distance flowering shrubs, such as roses, potentillas and cistus, can produce the same spotted effect with their small, disc-like flowers.

Using Distinctive Foliage The patterns that are created by distinctive foliage are invaluable in the garden because the effects last much longer than those of flowers. Leaf shapes can be rounded, slim, long, stubby or classically ovate and there are also even arrow- or heart-shaped leaves. The fine detailing of certain leaf shapes also creates patterns, whether because they are incised, twinned or fanned from a central point.

As always the grasses and reed-like leaves are an important part of this foliage mix, bringing clarity to other foliage patterns and creating striped patterns in the border. The tall, slim *Crocosmia* 'Golden Fleece' and the petite, striped *C.* 'Jackanapes' are good examples. I am also partial to the stiff patterns of *Sisyrinchium striatum* and the more lax, shining curves of *Hemerocallis* which should be grown *en masse* drifting among other sun-lovers like *Agastache foeniculum* and some levelling *Achillea* 'Anthea'.

Narrow, willow-like foliage is elegant, floating on the breeze and always in motion. The willows are the leaders with slimline leaves that overlap decoratively and lighten solid plants such as viburnums or static rhododendrons. The invasive but exquisite willow *Salix exigua* looks wonderful

in a rural garden viewed from a distance, perhaps combined with dogwoods or shrub elders. The weeping silver pear (*Pyrus salicifolia* 'Pendula'), a small grey-leaved tree with willow-like leaves, is also silvery and grown for its foliage rather than for its blossom. Not all willow-like leaves are so active. The leaves of *Cotoneaster salicifolius* and *Aucuba japonica* 'Salicifolia', for example, are rigid but their slimline form is invaluable for adding interest to less distinguished leaf shapes.

The finely detailed pattern created by a mass of tiny leaves is also a strong feature of shrubs. The tiny leaves of *Cotoneaster horizontalis*, with their fishbone pattern, naturally decorate the fanning habit of this useful wall shrub. Incidentally, you can exploit the different growth patterns of these plants to create an illusion of space in a small garden. By placing larger foliage patterns in the foreground you make plants seem closer than they really are while smaller foliage patterns appear further away. For example, the massed tiny leaves of *Cotoneaster conspicuus* would seem farther away than the larger, simpler leaves of *C. frigidus*.

If style is the order of the day, the leaves of the regally tall Indian poke (*Veratrum viride*) take some beating. This and its siblings *V. nigrum* and *V. album* provide rich green foliage once established from which tall striking flowers emerge. In moist, shaded conditions the uniquely pleated leaves are highly decorative, particularly if seen with the crinkled-leaved bronze *Rodgersia aesculifolia*, the softer *Alchemilla mollis* and a carpet of *Saxifraga fortunei* 'Rubrifolia'.

I should also refer the reader to the decorative value of variegated leaves. Make a point of looking for variegated plants because they offer a lightness of touch among the more sombre evergreens. Here again the cotoneasters have an offering. The leaves of *Cotoneaster horizontalis* 'Variegatus' have white edges that turn pink in autumn. This happens to a few variegated plants including members of the *Euonymus* family such as the low-growing *E. fortunei* 'Emerald Gaiety' and to *Fuchsia magellanica* 'Versicolor'. The latter is one of the finest fuchsias because its grey-green leaves have copper-pink overtones from which hang crimson and purple flowers.

Many shrubs also have variegated forms including the strawberry plant (*Fragaria*) and the extremely beautiful *Cornus alba* 'Elegantissima'. *C. a.* 'Spaethii' is equally sought after for the golden variegation that turns pink towards the end of the season. I am also reminded of two particularly beautiful forms of *Iris pallida*. *I. p.* 'Argentea Variegata' is striped pure white with grey and *I. p.* 'Aurea Variegata' has golden variegated leaves. There are also some variegated ground-covering plants that will bring pattern and light into shaded places. They include the variegated ivies, acid-loving *Pachysandra terminalis* 'Variegata' and a variegated form of ground elder that is not as ineradicable as its parent.

Top right
From a distance this garden in evening light is low in colour, composed of different tints of white, green and silver. Its charm lies in the great variety of textures and patterns that blend and contrast.

Right
The pinkish-orange flowers of tiger lilies (*Lilium lancifolium*), which appear from summer to early autumn, create a warm-coloured note in a border that is dominated by foliage plants such as jagged-leaved artichokes and layering hosta leaves as well as some attractive primulas.

Using Dramatic Leaf Shapes Huge leaves are a law unto themselves, dominating the garden so that neither texture nor pattern matter as much as the overall leaf shape. The mixture of rounded and sharp shapes, linear curves, massed spots and hazy effects need some impact to draw the eye to specific areas. Dramatic leaves fulfil this need, bringing a sense of order to garden patterns that is easily 'read' and yet rivetingly stylish.

incut, coarsely puckered and can reach up to 2 m (6½ ft) tall. There is also a selection of smaller, dramatically leaved plants that can be associated in the same moist landscape. These include the large, rounded leaves of the umbrella plant (*Darmera peltata*, syn. *Peltiphyllum peltata*), a mere 35 cm (14 in) across, and the paddle-shaped leaves of the skunk cabbage (*Lysichiton americanus*) which are 1.2 m (4 ft) wide, both of

which look good with the vertical contrast provided by the yellow flag iris (*Iris pseudacorus*).

The rounded leaves of *Astilboides tabularis* (syn. *Rodgersia tabularis*) can reach 90 cm (3 ft) in diameter. They are neither scalloped nor incut and are lighter green than their peers, so in both capacities they are distinctive. The highly invasive *Petasites japonicus giganteus* echoes this rounded leaf pattern elsewhere but it should not

If you garden in dry, sunny conditions there are few giant-leaved plants to choose from except for *Crambe cordifolia* with its cabbage-like leaves and tiny, gypsophila-like flowers and rather greyish foliage plants including *Macleaya cordata*, *Cynara cardunculus* and the luxuriant, jade-green *Melianthus major*. This is because most plants with large leaves require a fair amount of moisture and will grow best by pools or streams. The 1.5 m (5 ft) wide leaves of *Gunnera manicata* are

Above left

The huge leaves of this *Gunnera manicata* have unfurled early in the season and clearly dominate the planting at the water's edge.

Above centre

Distinctly shaped foliage like that of the cardoon (*Cynara cardunculus*) makes decorative silver patterns that look well with *Salvia pratensis*.

Above right

Simply shaped rounded leaves of *Ligularia dentata* 'Desdemona' beside *Hosta sieboldiana elegans* contrast with feathery *Acer palmatum dissectum*.

be allowed to rampage. In addition, the magnificent royal fern (*Osmunda regalis*) is also suited to pond edges where it unrolls elegant, decorative fronds in spring. These plants contrast well with the sculptural structure of other grand dames.

Rodgersias, ligularias and hostas also have much textural and decorative value. Their beautifully formed, large leaves are ideal for smaller gardens in damp soils. *Rodgersia podophylla* is bronzed while *Ligularia dentata* 'Desdemona' has dark reddish colouring. *R. sambucifolia* and *R. pinnata* both have pinnate foliage, which has great decorative impact, while *L.* 'The Rocket' has triangular, fringe-edged leaves. The spring-green ostrich fern (*Matteuccia struthiopteris*) would also be in scale at 90 cm (3 ft) tall.

Hostas have a perfection of form that is tidy, nearly symmetrical and generously lush although the variety of colours including greens, blues and

Hedera helix 'Manda's Crested' or lacy, richly textured astilbe leaves, the inevitable companion of the smooth, linear clarity of the hosta.

If you are drawn to exotic foliage, hardy palms such as the Chusan palm (*Trachycarpus fortunei*) can co-exist in temperate gardens with yuccas, cordylines and bamboos. Putting these powerful shapes together creates a dramatically spiky pattern. Hardier plants such as fatsias, acanthus

and phormiums also suit this exotic style. Phormiums are particularly accommodating plants if you garden in cooler places, their strong, sword-like leaves ideal for creating a highly striking pattern. They come in a variety of colours including green, reddish or variegated. For example, the strongly dominant grey swords of *Phormium tenax* can be successfully combined with the equally tall and imposing *Melianthus major*.

yellows should also be explored. The huge *Hosta sieboldiana elegans* is magnificently layered with ribbed, almost leathery, grey-blue leaves. Rich patterns can be created by siting it with the bronze, puckered leaves of *Rodgersia podophylla* backed by ferns. The similarly coloured *H.* 'Blue Angel' has fatter, deeply ridged leaves whereas those of *H.* 'Blue Wedgwood' are sharply pointed. The waxy surface of *H. undulata* creates rippled patterns that can be echoed by ground-covering

Above left
The orange-edged, green leaves of *Phormium tenax* 'Aurora' are dramatically sword-like.
Above centre
A richly decorative pattern is produced by the large leaves of *Heracleum mantegazzianum*, with their sharp, jagged edges, which rather resemble those of giant cow parsley.
Above right
This skunk cabbage (*Lysichiton americanus*) develops massive, paddle-shaped leaves as the season progresses provided it is grown in wet soil.

In a slightly warmer climate, other suitable companions with strongly shaped leaves include the giant reed (*Arundo donax*), the ginger lily (*Hedychium densiflorum*), *Dicksonia antarctica* and taller bamboos such as *Phyllostachys nigra*. Bamboos can be grown in cooler countries if they are protected in the winter and can be associated with the banana (*Musa basjoo*), cordylines and cannas, which are also topped with similarly dramatic orange flowers.

A Grass Garden The background to this garden is composed of the stiff, evergreen common or Norway spruce (*Picea abies*). These fast-growing conifers have needle-like leaves and can grow up to 20-30 m (70-100 ft) tall. As well as providing a dark-coloured canvas from which the plants in the border are launched, they establish a degree of stability for this wonderfully textured planting plan.

The overall design of the garden is calming with subtly coloured grasses and other grass-like foliage shapes repeated systematically throughout the border. There is also a variety of different textures that simply invite human touch. Indeed, many of the plants are highly tactile such as the fountain grass (*Pennisetum alopecuroides*, syn. *P. compressum*) whose flowers may be described as furry caterpillars clinging to the end of a fishing line as they sway in the wind. These flowers can become almost transparent in certain types of light when the very fine hairs are silhouetted. There are also other forms of fountain grass to choose from including tuft-forming *P. setaceum* (syn. *P. rueppellii*) and *P. villosum* (syn. *P. longistylum*) which has long stems and creamy pink flower heads in the autumn that fade to pale brown.

At the back of the border there other insubstantial flowers belonging to the decorative grasses *Miscanthus sinensis* and *M. sacchariflorus*. These are taller than the fountain grasses and so require more space. They are vigorous herbaceous grasses that spread slowly but eventually make strong clumps of reflexed foliage from which develop feathery sprays of silvered or pinkish-brown flowers. Similarly the silken plumes of a small pampas grass (*Cortaderia selloana* 'Pumila'), which is a rather elegant evergreen, also accentuate the mass of textural flowers. In late summer the silvery flower panicles, which can grow up to 60 cm (2 ft) long, are produced above arching, rather sharp-edged leaves.

The rest of the planting scheme provides contrasts of form and texture that emphasize the mobile lightness of the flowers. Stately mounds of grassy foliage also serve as an anchor for these fine, feathery textures. The

sharply attendant, sword-shaped leaves of evergreen New Zealand flax (*Phormium tenax* Purpureum Group) has a similar role. It is this orderliness that acts as a stabilizing balance in the overall plan.

A contrast of shape and leaf form is provided by flattened flower heads of *Sedum* 'Herbstfreude'. This clump-forming perennial has oval, fleshy, greyish leaves and pink flowers in late summer. The leaves also provide another very tactile texture, being smooth and velvet-surfaced. As the autumn progresses, the deep brown-red colour of this sedum will intensify. Wine-red S. 'Ruby Glow' has firm gritty leaves while the almost bristly foliage of the silvery, evergreen curry plant (*Helichrysum italicum*) also contributes a strongly static mass. The aptly named Michaelmas daisy (*Aster laterifolius* 'Horizontalis'), whose foliage can turn copper-purple in the autumn, and the invaluable blue *A.* x *frikartii* 'Mönch' have lighter textures and attractive, daisy-like flowers in late summer.

Spring

Spring, right After winter when the dead leaves have been cut back to base, a border such as this will be slow to start. So some small bulbs could be planted in order to fill in the spaces until the new summer greenness takes over. Bulbs such as green-and-white-flowered *Ornithogalum nutans* and small, deep blue *Scilla siberica* will eventually cover any bare earth. Evergreens and clipped helichrysum are as static as the sedums while the leaves of the neatly mounding *Ajania pacifica* (syn. *Chrysanthemum pacificum*) accentuate its overlapping, rosette habit.

Late autumn/winter, right The glory of the late season can be extended into winter. The colours of the border become almost monochrome, dominated by bleached straws, parchments and reddy browns. The leaves of the grasses may be dead but are still beautiful, preserved in form and edged with frost or laden with snow. Small evergreens at the front add texture and form while deep brown sedums provide smooth textural contrasts to the other papery, rustling textures. The late-flowering kaffir lily (*Schizostylis coccinea*) produces red flowers until Christmas. *Buddleja davidii* 'Black Knight' has been cut back in late autumn.

Summer, below The true style of this border is revealed in mid-summer when the tall, flowing foliage catches the breeze. A short time later, as summer progresses, the border is at its best when flower textures stir the whole scene.

Late Autumn/Winter

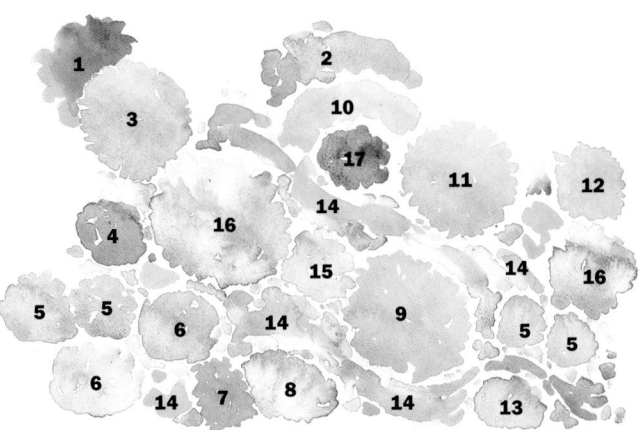

KEY *(H = Height; S = Spread)*

1. *Buddleja davidii* 'Black Knight', *H and S: 5 m (16 ft)*
2. *Rosa* x *odorata* 'Mutabilis', *H and S: 3 m (10 ft)*
3. *Cortaderia selloana* 'Pumila', *H: 2.5 m (8 ft); S: 1.2 m (4 ft)*
4. *Aster* x *frikartii* 'Mönch', *H: 75 cm (2½ ft); S: 45 cm (1½ ft)*
5. *Sedum* 'Herbstfreude', *H and S: 60 cm (2 ft)*

6. *Helichrysum italicum*, *H: 60 cm (2 ft); S: 90 cm (3 ft)*
7. *Ajania pacifica*, *H and S: 45 cm (1½ ft)*
8. *Sedum* 'Ruby Glow', *H and S: 45 cm (1½ ft)*
9. *Pennisetum alopecuroides*, *H: 90 cm (3 ft); S: 45 cm (1½ ft)*
10. *Aster lateriflorus* 'Horizontalis', *H: 60 cm (2 ft); S: 45 cm (1½ ft)*
11. *Miscanthus sacchariflorus*, *H: 2.5 m (8 ft); S: 90 cm (3 ft)*

12. *Miscanthus sinensis* 'Morning Light', *H: 1.2 m (4 ft); S: 45 cm (1½ ft)*
13. *Artemisia alba* 'Canescens', *H and S: 30 cm (1 ft)*
14. *Scilla siberica*, *H: 10-15 cm (4-6 in); S: 5 cm (2 in)*
15. *Ornithogallum nutans*, *H: 15-35 cm (6-14 in); S: 8-10 cm (3-4 in)*
16. *Phormium tenax* Purpureum Group, *H: 3 m (10 ft); S: 90-180 cm (3-6 ft)*
17. *Berberis thunbergii* 'Bagatelle', *H and S: 30 cm (1 ft)*
18. *Schizostylis coccinea* 'Major', *H: 60 cm (2 ft); S: 23-30 cm (9-12 in)*

COLOUR

Colour is one of life's deepest pleasures, rendering mood, seducing the eye and clearly indicating the seasons. Companions in colour are an ideal when putting plants together and can create harmonious, tranquil, dramatic or exciting effects in the garden. But as we learn more it becomes clear that there can be few absolutes with colour.

Hues are not constant, tonal relationships are not stable and 'rules' on colour harmony are flexible. This is partly because our perceptions of colour are personal so that the essence of a colour alters accordingly. The physical closeness of other colours can also cause apparent mutations while other changes occur because of the fleeting nature of light. Gardeners who explore the possibilities of colour can add new dimensions to the garden.

Left
This border is based on reds provided by crocosmias, potentillas, dahlias and penstemons with orange achilleas and red-foliaged berberis.

Above
Pink *Dierama pulcherrimum* and *Schizostylis coccinea* 'Mrs Hegarty' blend well with silvery artemisias, white campanulas and gypsophila.

AN INTRODUCTION TO COLOUR THEORY

We accept colour as a function of light; that is, radiant energy transmitted in wavelengths. Sir Isaac Newton discovered that a ray of light bends when it passes through glass or drops of water. (Remember as a child noticing how a stick seems to bend in a stream.) This light ray is also composed of different wavelengths of colour, splitting into a rainbow effect known as the spectrum.

primary colours but, left unmodified, they can be rather harsh and unsubtle. However, by mixing up these three colours you can create the other colours of the spectrum that are known as the secondary colours. So red merges into yellow to create orange; yellow melts into blue to produce green; and blue merges with red to make violet. The three secondary hues are therefore orange, green and violet.

Further to this, the three secondary colours have a tense relationship with the three primary colours. It has been observed that when each primary colour is placed beside an even mix of the other two, to create a secondary colour, then this results in a powerful struggle for dominance to which the eye cannot easily adjust. These colour relationships are described as 'complementary'. So, pure red beside mid-green appears to 'jump'

Above
Bronze and purple *Iris* 'Kent Pride', *Heuchera* 'Rachel', *Erysimum* 'Bowles' Mauve' and aquilegias blend well with hazy bronze fennel.

Above
This white bed is filled with tulips, the delicate white flowers of variegated honesty (*Lunaria annua*), variegated hostas and *Alchemilla mollis*.

Above
Rich, chocolate-black aeoniums are beautifully displayed against retaining timber boards and are a sympathetic contrast with *Sedum cauticola*.

These colours are the familiar succession of red, orange, yellow, green, blue, indigo and violet.

Although I have said that the appreciation of colours is subjective there are clearly some aspects of colour that can be measured. Of all the colours in the spectrum there are three pure ones, red, yellow and blue, that dominate. They themselves cannot be made and they are known as the primary colours. The greatest contrasts are achieved in the garden when you use only the

The proportion of hue in each mix can also be varied to create other subtleties of colour. For example, there are greens that are limey and greens that lean towards turquoise. Similarly, red with a small amount of blue will look crimson, grading towards the wine colours, while if it contains some yellow then it looks scarlet and graduates to the rust-reds. We can revel in such subtleties in the garden (see 'The Influence of Tints and Tones', on pages 74-77).

while blue adjoining orange or yellow next to violet have the same agitated result. The eye finds these combinations uncomfortable and copes by 'seeing' a white line between the two, separating them like wilful children.

So our perceptions are influential in how we see colours and our rational understanding of a colour is altered by the situation in which we actually see it. There are paradoxes here. Every colour is itself only in isolation. As soon as another colour is placed within the same visual field, the first colour seems different. It has not really changed but its companion affects its appearance. So placing colours together will modify them in some way. As I have already described, placing the complementary colours in close association can set up fierce competitions. In contrast, if you juxtapose colours that have a close affinity in the rainbow or spectrum such as

Below

Informally planted, this garden contains a diverse range of colours, in various tints and tones, including purple, lilac, red, pink, blue, yellow and white. The garden almost resembles the collection of colours on a painter's palette and contains a host of delicious, summer-flowering plants. These include the delicate, purple-blue flowers of campanulas as well as spherical, purple allium flowers, poppies, potentillas and monardas, all backed by dark green foliage.

red and orange or blue and green you can literally intensify the impact of each of the colours. Although gardeners are not painters, exploring these colour effects can be great fun because every colour has the ability to change the physical appearance of its neighbour. When planning our gardens we need to consider what effects we would like to create in the garden and then use the colours of foliage and flowers to achieve this.

THE EFFECTS OF LIGHT AND SHADE

One of the first things you should consider when choosing the colours for your garden is what areas of light and shade you have. Differing light levels affect the types of plant that you can grow as well as the colours that look most effective.

Shade is definitely an asset in the garden, acting rather like an oasis when the garden is exposed to brilliant light. The dark, mysterious havens created by shade are welcoming and there are many beautiful plants that revel in such protection. One of my great regrets is that most large-leaved, green foliage plants that work well together visually need damp soils and shady protection from drying heat. So the lush greenery of Irish planting is not possible for every site.

Shade-loving plants include many old faithfuls such as the ground-covering, glossy, round-leaved bergenias beside heart-shaped brunnera foliage. Another attractive scheme might also include the sword-leaved Gladwin iris (*Iris foetidissima*) with its modest pale yellow flowers and brilliant orange winter fruits as well as the grassy green *Liriope muscari* that carries rich purple flowers later in the year. You could also consider adding

Above left

Soft, pastel colours beneath this small tree, with its chocolate-brown bark, are provided by blue *Corydalis flexuosa* 'Père David', pink tiarella, yellow feverfew (*Tanacetum parthenium*), grassy *Molinia caerulea* and some variegated Jacob's ladder (*Polemonium*).

Left

Brightly coloured rhododendrons and azaleas, ranging from golden yellow to scarlet red to pale pink, are ideal for providing strong colours even in woodland conditions. Here, the different effects created by both the strong sunlight and the dappled light are highly pronounced.

the all-purpose *Alchemilla mollis* to soften the scheme with its slightly sage-coloured leaves and lime-green flowers. You might like to add some vincas and lamiums to add smaller patterns and varieties of colour in foliage and flower. Vincas have white, blue and magenta-purple flowers while lamiums also come in cream. These are all flower colours that work well together. Most gardens have a shaded area and here paler colours come into their own, glowing far more than if they were bleached out in bright sunshine. In fact, by late evening pale colours gain in strength and density of hue, becoming almost fluorescent.

There is an increased choice of plants for dappled light that have good leaf textures and flower colours although again many prefer moist soils. Here, ferns, astilbes, solomon's seal (*Polygonatum biflorum*) and acid-loving ground-covers like *Asarum europaeum* and *Maianthemum bifolium* have a green lushness. A subtle colour scheme for spring might combine lime-green *Euphorbia amygdaloides robbiae* with green-and-white hellebores, blue brunneras, omphalodes, columbines and bluebells. This could be followed by violet-blue *Aconitum* 'Bressingham Spire', pink, red or white astilbes and sculptured hostas with their

lilac and white flower spikes. Later on the white or pink hybrid *Anemone hupehensis* 'September Charm' or *A.* x *hybrida* 'Honorine Jobert' could glow among densely dark rhododendron foliage .

If you prefer bright colours in light shade and you have acidic soil, then the rhododendrons are unbeatable. The hybrids have cool-toned flowers, so cool pinks, purples and crimsons dominate. In contrast, the flower colours of deciduous azaleas are hotter, being gold- or orange-based. So, some care should be exercised when planting them together. Suitable partners for both are ferns, bluebells, hellebores, anemones and foxgloves.

Below

These pale pink and white forms of *Helleborus orientalis* are associated with the dainty, white snowdrops (*Galanthus*) and seem to glow in the reduced light that occurs at the edge of the woodland.

Below

There is a wide variety of green tints to choose from when planting a foliage garden; here black-leaved *Ophiopogon planiscapus* 'Nigrescens' is combined with hostas, astrantias, creeping ivies and bugle.

If you have a sun-filled garden with little shade, wind will be as much of a problem as dryness. Once you have accounted for constraints such as these there is a large choice of plants. Bear in mind that intense light is ideal for setting off primary colours and the saturated colours that come from them. Although the entire colour spectrum is available for hot, sunny sites remember that the form and shape of the plants should play a controlling role in a kaleidoscopic effect (see 'Fairground Colour', on pages 104-5).

Given this, you might try a colour scheme based upon harmonious linking so that reds and yellows are held together with oranges and the occasional dot of midnight blue. Consider crocosmias, helianthemums, rudbeckias, kniphofias, monardas and salvias with a renegade deeply blue *Veronica austriaca teucrium* 'Crater Lake Blue' for fun. Alternatively, purple, violet or blue could be linked using columbines, anchusas, campanulas, perovskias, delphiniums and alliums. You could include challengers such as *Euphorbia griffithii* 'Fireglow' or a copper helenium. If you prefer complementary colours (see page 68) rather than harmonious ones I suggest a golden or pale yellow border with blue touches. Yellow-leaved *Philadelphus coronarius* 'Aureus' and *Milium effusum* 'Aureum' with blue geraniums or campanulas might continue the theme.

Where we live also influences our colour preferences because latitude affects the colours of the plants that are familiar to us. Northern light tends to be bluer which moderates flower colour and favours subtle hues. As you near the equator the light becomes more yellow, and calls for stronger flower colours. These regional variations are obvious when plants from hotter climates are used in temperate zones as bedding beause they look too bright beside gently coloured natives.

Open garden areas are subject to changing light levels throughout the day and the seasons which affect the intensity of colour. In the morning, colours are at their most intense which is why film actors appear on set so early. By midday, the light is so strong that it reduces the intensity, and different parts of the garden become appealing. By the evening the light is more subdued with pastels and whites looking positively luminous. Clearly light changes the appearance of everything and colour is far more than merely pretty.

Above left

The delicate colour combination in this border comes from pink *Monarda* 'Cherokee', mauve thalictrum, silvery *Eryngium giganteum* and *Calamagrostis* x *acutifolia* which blend together harmoniously in the afternoon sunshine.

Left

This border is exactly the same as the one above but the photograph is taken much later in the day when the warm evening light bathes the plants. They have been specifically chosen to benefit from the varying light levels. The grassy textures of many of the plants seem to glow with colour while silver flower heads of the eryngiums are luminous.

Top near right

Evening light glows amid delphiniums and poppies, mingled with *Rosa* 'Fred Loads', *R.* 'Iceberg' and *R.* 'The Queen Elizabeth'.

Top far right

A cool cream form of *Iris germanica* and *Rosa* 'Frühlingsgold' enliven this muted scheme of blue and lilac aquilegias and wine-red *Rosa rugosa*.

Bottom near right

Soft light strengthens the colour of blue petunias, red pelargoniums, pink dahlias and purple salvias.

Bottom far right

Warm evening light intensifies the colour of red nasturtiums, dahlias and orange lilies.

THE INFLUENCE OF TINTS AND TONES

Colour has many decorative qualities but it can also contribute to mood and create apparent temperature changes. Dramatic effects can also be created using heat-generating scarlets and oranges or calm-inducing cool blues.

The emotive effects of colour are recognized in all cultures, the temperature of the hues having a direct influence upon our emotional response to the garden around us. We all acknowledge the warming effects of sunny yellows, fire-like reds and hot oranges and the coolness of blues and violets. Colours such as red are insistent and exciting and, in association with other

vermilion *Lychnis chalcedonica* or the rich orange of *Asclepias tuberosa*. Similarly an association of Flanders red poppies (*Papaver rhoeas*) with blue flax (*Linum narbonense*) creates a cooler effect than poppies among yellow wheat where the redness becomes a sunny, inviting scarlet.

Colour has another powerful influence on our perceptions. Hot colours can appear closer while blue and violet hues seem to recede. Centuries ago landscape painters used this to give their work depth, toning down distant objects by adding blue to the natural colour. In the same way, borders that are bluer in hue seem to retreat and increase the apparent depth.

Left

Here is a garden composed of the cool colour of blueish-pink achilleas, white *Lysimachia clethroides* and filipendulas which are combined with warm-coloured orange lilies, alstroemeria, heleniums and red poppies.

Above

Amaranthus caudatus is planted with penstemons, montbretias and rudbeckia.

Above left

Dahlias, astrantias and nasturtiums are combined with plum *Plantago* foliage.

powerful colours, red can look sensational. Artists are familiar with this manipulation of colours to create an emotional impact or swing a mood. But they take things further and play with our responses. For example, while mid-red may be described as 'hot', red can also seem 'cold' when mixed with blue such as in *Rosa* 'William Lobb' and *Fuchsia* 'Tom Thumb'. Conversely mixing the same red with yellow will warm it. Look at the heated hues of the

The colours of the spectrum tend to be either naturally dark or light so that photographed with a black-and-white film we see the lighter yellows as almost white and the purples as virtually black. In terms of painting this natural order can be altered by adding white to produce pastels or darkening a colour to deepen its value. So there are creamy yellows and dark ochre yellows, pale lilacs and deeper purples. We may select pinks, jade greens and pale blues or choose maroons, dark greens or midnight blue. If you plant pale shades against a dark background or deep ones in a light-filled scene the effect is striking in the garden.

Although contrast is a useful tool when associating plants it is not the only one. Harmonizing similar tints is another attractive device. It is interesting to compare two Californian plants here. The shrub *Carpenteria californica* has dark green leaves that contrast sharply with the delicately white flowers. On the other hand, the white flowers of the Californian tree poppy (*Romneya coulteri*) arise from pale, blue-green leaves. In this case the white is reinforced by a harmonic relationship with similarly pale-toned leaves.

Harmonies of similarly deepened or lightened shades, albeit of different colours, can also intensify the effect of each. Brilliantly red canna flowers look stunning emerging from their dark, bronzed foliage while scarlet *Lobelia* 'Queen Victoria' also blends in with its deep green-brown leaves. A similar emphasis can be achieved by placing dark flowers against dark foliage. So indigo-blue monkshood (*Aconitum napellus*) will be enriched by the plum-red leaves of *Cotinus coggygria*. In the same way paler shades can be

used together. Their tonal value may be similar but the impact of the colours is more concentrated resulting in positively luminous schemes.

The fine tuning of the colours can create simple, exquisite effects. Pastels in particular have an almost indefinable subtlety that suits the romantic garden style and yet can lighten the solemnity of a formal garden. Choose your plants to harmonize within a similar tonal range such as creamy, silver-leaved *Achillea* 'Anthea' and the ivory-coloured *Lupinus arboreus*. Even pale green combinations can be devised using white flowers tinted with green, such as spring-flowering *Helleborus argutifolius*, *Veratrum viride*, *Eucomis comosa* and *Kniphofia* 'Green Jade', to blend with nearby flowers and foliage.

The light levels in different seasons can also affect colour intensity, the yellows, pale blues and pinks of spring giving way to the hot colours of high summer and eventually to the fires of autumn. Fruits and autumn leaves will provide warmth before the more chill colours of winter appear such as green, pale pink and creamy yellow hellebores and a few cream, yellow and pale pink winter-flowering shrubs that do not need to compete with the technicolour of summer.

Top right
Mahogany-coloured sneezeweeds (*Helenium*) are combined here with copper *Achillea* 'Feuerland'.
Centre right
Climbing *Rosa* 'American Pillar' mingles with claret-red *Clematis* 'Madame Julia Correvon' and light blue *Campanula lactiflora*.
Bottom right
Coneflowers (*Echinacea purpurea*), with their dark centres, provide a lilac-pink contrast with rust-red *Helenium* 'Kupferzwerg' and dark red *Achillea* 'Summerwine'.

Top right
This blue and yellow colour scheme contains campanulas with anthemis in the background.
Top far right
Subtly coloured, this bed is based on cream, yellow and a touch of grey and includes kniphofias, santolinas and angelica.
Right
Flame-red flowers of *Crocosmia* 'Lucifer' are magnificent with apricot lilies and tawny orange *Achillea* 'Feuerland' and contrast with the foaming lime-yellow flowers of *Alchemilla mollis*.

COLOUR

Right
Deep, plum-coloured foliage of *Cotinus coggygria* 'Royal Purple' flatters the variegated foliage of *Euonymus fortunei* 'Emerald Gaiety' and the soft pink flowers of *Sedum spectabile*.

Below
A dramatically beautiful border is planted with silvery artemisias and elegant, feather-textured *Helichrysum* which provide the perfect garden canvas for these scarlet dahlias, lobelias and potentillas. The whole bed looks still more delightful backed by the solid dark green hedge.

Near right
Dark red cotinus and variegated dogwood (*Cornus alba* 'Elegantissima') provide a striking background for purple-bronze irises.

Centre right
Purple-leaved *Cercis canadensis* 'Forest Pansy' and *Heuchera* 'Palace Purple' with red roses, monardas, orange achilleas and pink *Dierama pulcherrimum* are set off by silver *Pyrus salicifolia* 'Pendula'.

Far right
Tulips attract the eye in front of the yellow-splashed foliage of *Ilex* x *altaclerensis* 'Lawsoniana'.

THE GARDEN CANVAS

In temperate areas green foliage nearly always forms the background from which other colours are launched. In damper latitudes, green hues create a lush, soil-covering backcloth. Inevitably this affects all the other colours in the garden. Green implies a great range of mutated hues varying from yellow-lime *Philadelphus coronarius* 'Aureus' to turquoise-blue *Ruta graveolens* 'Jackman's Blue'. Choosing the right shade of green foliage will affect the way you perceive the colour of any near companions (see page 68-9).

The effect of most variegated foliage is to lighten the look of the planted area and to add vitality to the colour canvas. Dogwoods like *Cornus alba*

to be dark green foliage such as *Viburnum tinus* or *V. davidii* against which pale blue *Geranium pratense* 'Mrs. Kendall Clark' might glow.

In full sun the mid-greens of most perennial foliage will form a tranquil backdrop to the kaleidoscope of flower colours. But this does not work everywhere. In hot, dry countries it is silver-grey foliage that is used to blend the other colours. In the absence of rain, grey is the 'poor man's green'. There are many plants with silver or grey leaves such as *Melianthus major* that will provide a soothing foil for the bolder colour relationships.

Silver- and blue-foliaged plants are also flattering among pastel planting schemes because they prevent them from becoming pallid and unexciting.

'Elegantissima' and *Weigela florida* 'Aureovariegata' are ideal background shrubs. There are also variegated hostas and brunnera for shade and variegated grasses for sunnier areas. Many irises are in fact enhanced by their own white-striped leaves. Of particular value as a background planting are dark-leaved plants such as yews or Portugal laurel (*Prunus lusitanica*) and pale shrubs like *Pittosporum tenuifolium* 'James Stirling' or the herbaceous fleshy leaves of *Sedum spectabile*. These contrasts of light with dark are invaluable when you want to simplify a scheme. Look at the levels of light in the garden and then decide whether you want to create dramatic contrasts or peaceful harmony. For example, in areas of dappled shade there is likely

They include feathery artemisias, woolly *Stachys byzantina*, grassy *Festuca glauca* 'Elijah Blue', ferny *Santolina chamaecyparissus*, satin *Convolvulus cneorum*, waxen blue hostas and tall shrubs that flicker with silver such as *Elaeagnus angustifolia* Caspica Group, *Pyrus salicifolia* 'Pendula', the pewter-grey foliage of the New Zealand daisy bush (*Olearia* x *macrodonta*) or the silvered sage-green *Rosa fedtschenkoana*. There are also plants with purple or reddish-brown foliage that can be used when planting a coloured border to link in with the colours of the flowers. These foliage plants can also be incorporated as part of a garden tapestry to add variety to the dominating greens, particularly when there are very few flowers to enliven a border.

SINGLE COLOUR SCHEMES

Every hue has unlimited permutations, whether pale or dark. Colours will be warm when red or golden yellow are mixed in or cool with blues and purples. Combining flower and foliage hues of the same colour can have great impact in the garden.

White All-white gardens have proliferated since the famous white garden at Sissinghurst Castle in Kent, England, was completed. Entrancing in summer when all about are losing their heads to the vivid feasting elsewhere there is a simple freshness in white flowers, particularly among green foliage. There are white forms of tulip, iris, lily, peony, lychnis, phlox, zantedeschia, leucanthemella, scabious, poppy and veronica whose effect en masse is wondrous. In white gardens silver and spring-green leaves and white-marked, glossy foliage provide a perfect launch. Different textures also create contrasting effects and it is by these subtleties that blandness is avoided.

Foliage in the white garden takes on a role equal to that of the flowers. It often acts as a foil; dark hedging, such as yew and holly, or dark red Prunus x cistena being very effective. The more informal mounds of dark foliaged shrubs such as deeply toned Sambucus nigra 'Guincho Purple' or round Fagus sylvatica 'Purpurea Pendula' are equally suitable. Good contrasts can also be achieved with evergreen shrubs including the darker Viburnum tinus and Prunus lusitanica.

The role of foliage is different when it emphasizes whiteness through harmony. This is where the silvery plants are so invaluable. Convolvulus cneorum and Anaphalis margaritacea are white-flowered plants with silvery foliage that literally carry their own harmonies with them. Some grey-leaved plants are almost white. These include Artemisia ludoviciana 'Valerie Finnis' with its young rosettes of nearly pure white leaves. A. stelleriana 'Nana' and A. alba 'Canescens' other white plants ideal for the front of the border.

Larger perennials such as the silvery, feathered A. ludoviciana 'Silver Queen' and the more grey-silver 60 cm (2 ft) tall shrub A. 'Powis Castle' can sit further back. Tall silver-jade Melianthus

Above
Crambe cordifolia, Campanula latiloba alba and Viola cornuta Alba Group glow in this low light.
Top near right
An all-white planting of tulips, roses and deutzia.
Top far right
A white hydrangea amid a show of white petunias.
Bottom near right
Late spring tulips planted in front of Viburnum x burkwoodii and fringed by white Myosotis.
Bottom far right
Rosa 'Jacqueline du Pré' planted with Crambe cordifolia and a young Onopordum acanthium.

major and smooth, grey Macleaya cordata will also grow in accord among the taller white perennials. All require sun and prefer well-drained soil.

These silvers also blend in with a hazy, white gypsophilas, daisy-flowered rhythmically vertical Veronicastrum virginicum album and Leucanthemum x superbum 'Snowcap' as well as Phlox paniculata 'White Admiral', the structured white lilies and agapanthus. They can be surrounded by seeded white valerian (Centranthus ruber albus) or drifts of sweet rocket (Hesperis matronalis). Many foliage plants such as santolinas and lavenders can be formally clipped. Others are more relaxed and spreading such as woolly stachys, the grassy leaves of pinks (Dianthus) and the velvety, pewter-coloured Salvia officinalis. All these associations are based on co-operation.

Many shrubs are variegated with white such as Cornus alba 'Elegantissima', Weigela 'Florida Variegata', evergreen Euonymus fortunei 'Silver Queen' and Rhamnus alaternus 'Argenteovariegata', all of which can be used as a background. Plants such as phormiums, irises and yuccas have white-striped, sword-like leaves that add pattern to white flowers. Remember that unless you have a gravelled garden with Mediterranean light then green is the usual backcloth; just think of white cosmos with its fresh green foliage.

The white garden is not really a 'dead' whiteness because white can be touched with a hint of other pale colours. You can also assimilate some very pale planting associates like milky cream Sisyrinchium striatum, powder-blue geraniums, campanulas and delphiniums, lavenders, pale apricots, blush pink Dianthus 'Doris' and also Gypsophila 'Veil of Roses'. Used sparingly these colours lift a white garden considerably.

A White Garden A white bed has great charm, revealing the shapes and patterns of the plants very clearly. Green and silver-grey foliage in this border also provides a link and a decorative foil for the flowers. Dark, glossy evergreen *Prunus laurocerasus* 'Otto Luyken' in particular provides a launch for the cool whites, gleaming silvers and fresh greens. The lapping patterns of the hostas are softened by the downy, frilled leaves of *Alchemilla mollis*. This grey theme is continued by dramatically spiny Scotch thistle (*Onopordum acanthium*) and by feathery, pewter-grey *Artemisia* 'Powis Castle' whose leaves flatter the white flowers as they emerge.

This border changes constantly from early spring through to summer and autumn. The structural plants such as prunus and perennial astrantias, hostas, artemisias, alchemillas and campanulas are planted early and gradually expand with the years. Bulbs and annual and biennial fillers are added twice a year to create first a spring focus and then a different summer effect.

Soil conditioning is also important in this bed when so many demands are constantly made by changing the plants. Fertilizing and maintaining a good soil texture will encourage healthy plant growth while planning ahead is essential with seeds sown in pots well in advance ready for transplanting.

Summer

Spring above The early flowers are supplied by the white winter pansies and the annual variegated honesty (*Lunaria annua* 'Alba Variegata'). The pure white, pincushion-like daisies, *Bellis perennis* 'Alba Plena', are grown as annually planted biennials. *Tulipa* 'Snowpeak' and the lily-shaped *T.* 'White Triumphator' add stature. Lower down a mass of white and blue forget-me-nots (*Myosotis alpestris*) act as spring fillers.

Summer, right The tulips have now been removed and the myosotis weeded away. Permanent *Elymus hispidus*, *Campanula latiloba*, *C. persicifolia* and the hostas have all filled out. The astrantias have pinkish-white flowers in bold clumps and the honesty has delicate, green, disc-like seedheads. Summer additions include tobacco plants (*Nicotiana alata*), white petunias and *Dianthus barbatus albus*, which are transplanted from earlier sowings.

Late summer/early autumn, right A space in the bed has been filled with a silver-grey *Artemisia ludoviciana* 'Silver Queen' planted in a container. The rather dramatic flowers of *Crinum* x *powellii* 'Album' appear above daisy-flowered marguerites, both of which have been transplanted from containers. Pale blue petunias replace the blue forget-me-nots while *Nicotiana alata* fills the spaces at the front. Dahlias are in full flower and the Scotch thistle (*Onopordum acanthium*) produces fluffy seed-heads that will be distributed to another site. Beautifully white, papery seeds of variegated honesty (*Lunaria annua* 'Alba Variegata') will survive most of the winter unless picked by a flower arranger for indoor display.

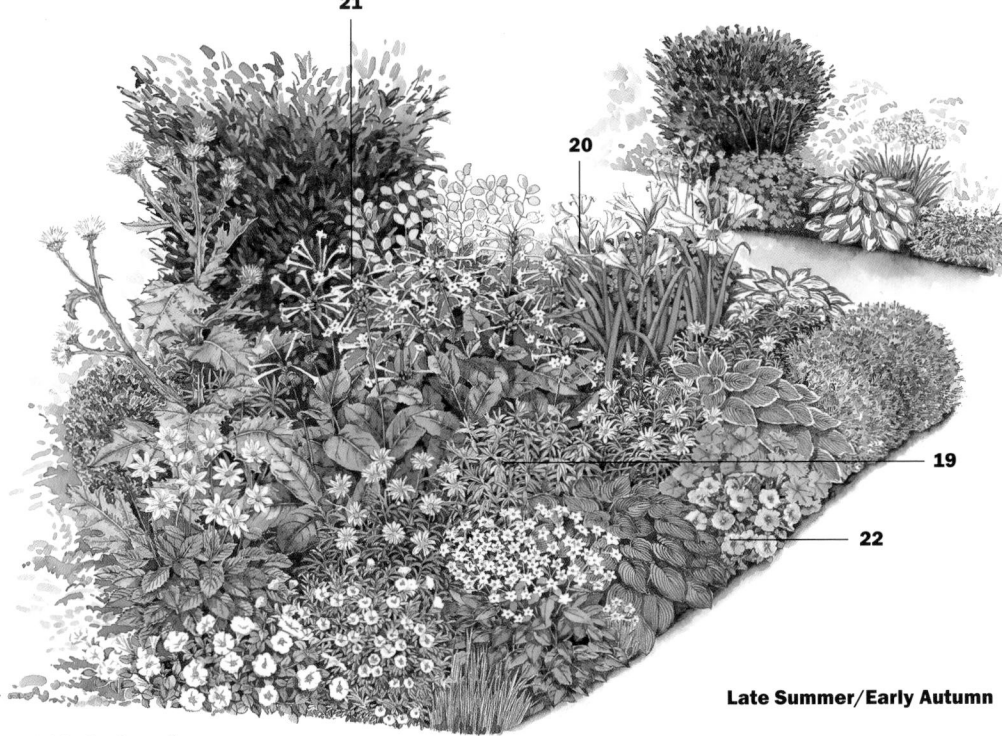

Late Summer/Early Autumn

KEY *(H = Height; S = Spread)*

1. *Agapanthus* 'Bressingham White', *H: 75 cm (2½ ft); S: 45 cm (1½ ft)*

2. *Elymus hispidus*, *H: 20 cm (8 in); S: 15 cm (6 in)*

3. *Alchemilla mollis*, *H and S: 50 cm (20 in)*

4. *Argyranthemum frutescens*, *H and S: 90 cm (3 ft)*

5. *Artemisia* 'Powis Castle', *H: 90 cm (3 ft); S: 1.2 m (4 ft)*

6. *Astrantia major involucrata*, *H: 60 cm (2 ft); S: 45 cm (1½ ft)*

7. *Campanula latiloba*, *H: 90 cm (3 ft); S: 45 cm (1½ ft)*

8. *Campanula persicifolia* 'Boule de Neige', *H: 90 cm (3 ft); S: 30 cm (1 ft)*

9. *Convolvulus cneorum*, *H and S: 75 cm (2½ ft)*

10. *Dahlia* Coltness hybrid, *H and S: 45 cm (1½ ft)*

11. *Dianthus barbatus albus*, *H: 45 cm (1½ ft); S: 30cm (1 ft)*

12. *Lunaria annua* 'Alba Variegata', *H: 75 cm (2½ ft); S: 30 cm (1 ft)*

13. *Hosta undulata albomarginata*, *H: 75 cm (2½ ft); S: 90 cm (3 ft)*

14. *Hosta sieboldiana*, *H: 90 cm (3 ft); S: 1.5 m (5 ft)*

15. *Nicotiana alata*, *H: 75 cm (2½ ft); S: 30 cm (1 ft)*

16. *Petunia* (white), *H: 15-30 cm (6-12 in); S: 30 cm (1 ft)*

17. *Prunus laurocerasus* 'Otto Luyken', *H: 90 cm (3 ft); S: 1.8 m (6 ft)*

18. *Onopordum acanthium*, *H: 1.8 m (6 ft); S: 90 cm (3 ft)*

19. *Artemisia ludoviciana* 'Silver Queen', *H: 90 cm (3 ft); S: 60 cm (2 ft)*

20. *Crinum* x *powellii* 'Album', *H: 90 cm (3 ft); S: 60 cm (2 ft)*

21. *Nicotiana sylvestris*, *H: 1.5 m (5 ft); S: 75 cm (2½ ft)*

22. *Petunia* (pale blue), *H: 15-30 cm (6-12 in); S: 30 cm (1 ft)*

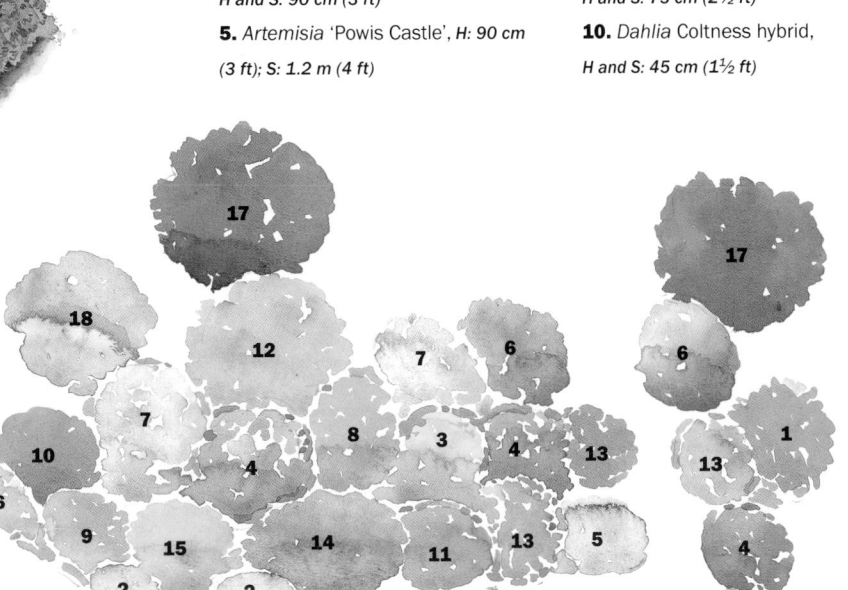

83

Yellow Lemons and sunshine are just a few of the images conjured up by the word yellow. An inviting colour, it has various effects on the garden. From a distance yellows are dominating and seem to advance forward. So when massed in a mixed border the yellow plants appear larger and closer than they really are. When planning a yellow border remember that it will be a focal point in the garden and other areas will be subservient. Thoughtless, random placing can upset the balance and create a restless effect.

Yellows can be put together without planning but the result may be jarring because yellow can either veer towards lime green and lemon or towards orange and gold. Two shrubs explain what I mean. *Philadelphus coronarius* 'Aureus' has butter-yellow leaves with lime-green tones while the leaves of *Spiraea japonica* 'Goldflame' are closer to orange than to green. These two shrubs should not be companions because they nullify one another. Far better to make each the foundation of a type of yellow association. So, look on yellow as two colours when you are making your plant selection. Of course, these are only suggested guidelines and the two can be used together but a link must be established by grey-blue or dark green foliage.

Warm yellows are found in winter-flowering witch hazels (*Hamamelis*) followed by yellow spring daffodils. Primroses do not associate as well because they are slightly tinged with green but try using the bright yellow, daisy-like flowers of leopard's bane (*Doronicum*). In summer, rudbeckias, inulas and many heliopsis continue the daisy theme. To balance the 'dotty' pattern, add some spiky red-hot pokers such as *Kniphofia caulescens*, tall goldenrod (*Solidago*) and the columnar loosestrife (*Lysimachia punctata*) as a contrast. The golden theme can be continued with *Hemerocallis* 'Golden Chimes' and some platelets of *Achillea* 'Coronation Gold'. Green leaves are cooling

---

SINGLE YELLOWS

Anthemis tinctoria 'E. C. Buxton'
An evergreen perennial with a height and spread of 90 cm (3 ft), ferny foliage and pale lemon flowers. It prefers well-drained soil and full sun.

Coreopsis 'Goldfink'
A hardy herbaceous dwarf perennial with a bushy habit and yellow, daisy-like flowers in summer. It has a height and spread of 30 cm (1 ft).

Forsythia 'Beatrix Farrand'
This is a deciduous, sun-loving, arching shrub which has golden flowers in the spring and a height and spread of 2 m (6½ ft).

Hemerocallis 'Stella de Oro'
This 40 cm (16 in) tall hardy herbaceous perennial has small, yellow, long-lasting flowers and spreads by 45 cm (1½ ft).

Ligularia 'The Rocket'
A perennial with tall flower spikes growing from black stems in midsummer. It has large, toothed leaves and requires semi-shade and a rich soil. It grows up to 1.5 m (5 ft) tall with a spread of 60 cm (2 ft).

Philadelphus coronarius 'Aureus'
A deciduous hardy shrub with bright yellow foliage that becomes lime green. It has fragrant white flowers in early summer and should be grown in light, dappled shade. It grows to 2.5 m (8 ft) with a spread of 1.5 m (5 ft).

Rudbeckia fulgida sullivantii 'Goldsturm'
This sun-loving herbaceous perennial has deep yellow, black-centred flowers which appear from late summer to autumn. It has a height and spread of 75 cm (2½ ft).

---

amid this warm splendour. Purple fennel and the soft, brown inflorescences of *Macleaya cordata* could also provide a colour link while white flowers and variegated foliage could be included with restraint.

Alternatively, the lemon yellows would provide a much cooler border. You can include daisy-flowered *Anthemis tinctoria* 'E. C. Buxton' and *A. t.* 'Wargrave' and *Argyranthemum* 'Jamaica Primrose' with primrose-yellow X *Solidaster luteus* 'Lemore' and the citrus-yellow *Kniphofia* 'Percy's Pride' for a contrast of form. Pale-citron *Hemerocallis* 'Whichford' and *Achillea* 'Moonshine' or *A.* 'Anthea' would also blend in.

These yellows are kinder to paler associates than the warmer ones and so pastel or cream flowers can be woven in. Yellow *Scabiosa ochroleuca* provides a small pattern among the foliage mass while the sulphur-coloured *Thalictrum lucidum* also works in well. Lower down cream-flowered *Sisyrinchium striatum* and *Helichrysum* 'Sulphur Light' might be included, while plants with silver and grey foliage can also be included in the scheme.

Top near right
This lovely yellow planting association contains a variety of different flower shapes including lythrums, osteospermums, stately lupins and daisies.
Bottom near right
In late summer this border display contains dahlias, the black-eyed, yellow flowers of rudbeckia and the feathery flowers of solidago.
Top far right
An effective single colour planting is devoted to a host of early flowering *Primula beesiana*, *P. bulleyana* and *P.* x *bulleesiana* in different shades of yellow.
Centre far right
This fresh spring planting contains a mass of ferns and golden-yellow daffodils.
Bottom far right
Warm orange-coloured *Alstroemeria* have been planted around an old-fashioned stone trough and seem to glow with strong, vibrant colour.

Red Although I have said that red is a hot, bold colour this is not always the case. Everything depends on whether the red is hot- or cool-toned. Scarlet reds that contain a trace of yellow are the blazing reds associated with flaming borders. But there are also reds of a more purple turn of mind that are crimson-cool. The difference is rather like that between a garnet and a ruby. By recognizing these subtleties your colour arrangement will not be thoughtless but carefully constructed for maximum effect.

A hot-toned red border glows with vitality and should include rust-reds as well as vermilions. The copper tones of *Helenium* 'Coppelia' or even the near orange of *H. hoopesii* 'Wyndley' beside the definitive scarlet of *Crocosmia* 'Lucifer', *Monarda* 'Cambridge Scarlet' and vermilion *Lychnis* x *arkwrightii* could be electrified by an adjacent mass of dark brick-orange *Kniphofia* 'Shining Sceptre'. Back these plants with shining, bronzed *Corylus maxima* 'Purpurea' or provide a clash with purple-leaved, wide-spreading *Cercis canadensis* 'Forest Pansy', both of which are dark toned. The scheme could also include the majestic sword-like forms of apricot-coloured *Phormium* 'Maori Sunrise' or bronze *P. tenax* Purpureum Group.

Top row
Left **Wine-red *Clematis* 'Niobe' amid cool pink *Rosa* 'Zéphirine Drouhin'.** Middle **Penstemon 'Garnet' with *Allium bollandicum* and *A. cernuum*.** Right **Crimson *Sedum dendroideum* planted beside a variegated agave.**
Middle row
Left **Scarlet and crimson dahlias, petunias, verbenas, sedums and antirrhinums.** Middle **Blood-red dahlias in late summer.** Right **Lilac-red *Rosa* 'Camaïeux', *Centranthus ruber* and *Stachys macrantha*.**
Bottom row
Left **Orange-red azaleas with *Rhododendron* 'Elizabeth'.** Middle **Dahlia 'Ellen Houston' and nasturtiums are equally fiery.** Right **Dahlia 'Bishop of Llandaff' planted with red berberis, penstemons, dianthus and kniphofia.**

SINGLE REDS

***Cornus florida* 'Cherokee Chief'**
A red-flowering dogwood with ruby bracts and outstanding autumn colour. It grows well in neutral to acid soil in sun or light shade, and has a height and spread of 2.5 m (8 ft).

***Cotinus coggygria* 'Royal Purple' (Smoke Tree)**
With a height and spread of 3 m (10 ft) this spreading deciduous shrub has purple-red foliage and hazy flowers. It prefers a well-drained, sunny site.

***Crocosmia* 'Lucifer'**
A hardy, bulbous, sun-loving perennial with tall, sword-shaped leaves. It has flame-coloured flower spikes in midsummer and grows to 90 cm (3 ft) tall with a spread of 20-25 cm (8-10 in).

***Euonymus europaeus* 'Red Cascade'**
A deciduous shrub that becomes rich red in autumn. The greenish flowers appear in late spring. It grows up to 3 m (10 ft) tall and 1.8 m (6 ft) wide.

***Helenium autumnale* (Sneezeweed)**
The daisy-like, mahogany-crimson flowers of this perennial appear in late summer. This sun-loving plant grows to 1.2 m (4 ft) tall with a spread of 45 cm (1½ ft).

***Imperata cylindrica* 'Red Baron' (Japanese Blood Grass)**
A spreading, red-leaved grass that grows to 35 cm (14 in) with a spread of 30 cm (1 ft). It prefers light shade or full sun and good drainage.

***Lychnis chalcedonica* (Maltese Cross)**
A perennial with scarlet summer flowers that prefers sun and good drainage. It grows to 90-120 cm (3-4 ft) tall with a spread of 30 cm (1 ft).

Association with dark red, brown and deep green foliage intensifies the colour range further. For example, *Lobelia cardinalis* has deep green leaves and *L.* 'Queen Victoria' has dark, reddened foliage. Copper-red *Heuchera* 'Palace Purple' and the bronzed, old-gold leaves of *Libertia peregrinans* might sit lower down. There are also hybrids of *Hemerocallis* and *Iris germanica* to reflect the tone of the other plants. Within this inferno I would also add a deep purple delphinium as a witty rejoinder.

Care is necessary when it comes to the cool-toned crimson reds. For example, a back-lit association of red *Berberis thunbergii atropurpurea* and *Cotinus coggygria* 'Royal Purple' is richly red but if light shines directly on the plants then the leaves look leaden and grey-blue in colour. This can be attractive if there are some carmine or deep pink flowers in the vicinity but too much of this colour has a dampening effect upon the spirits. Lighten the effect with plants like *Rosa glauca* with its purpled, dove-grey leaves and globe artichoke (*Cynara cardunculus* Scolymus Group) with its huge, jagged, silver leaves and mauve flowers.

Perennials such as *Phlox paniculata* 'Vintage Wine', *Lythrum salicaria* 'Firecandle' and *Echinacea purpurea* 'Magnus' stay within the cool, red-pink theme while *Geranium macrorrhizum* 'Bevan's Variety' and forms of *Centranthus ruber* also set the pace. *Knautia macedonica* adds spots of ruby while purple sage, *Euphorbia dulcis* 'Chameleon' and *Heucherella alba* 'Bridget Bloom' all blend at foot.

Claret colours need silver and grey foliage such as artemisias or *Pittosporum tenuifolium* 'Irene Paterson' at the back. Some restrained deep purple or pale blue avoids a dull look and creates a less fusty scheme. Crimson-red borders can also benefit from early red tulips and rich red, tender annuals such as dahlias, fuchsias, verbenas and nicotiana.

Blue Do the blues have to be sad? They are certainly quiet and soothing and contribute greatly to your experience of a garden. They affect your emotions and suggest peaceful tranquillity. Blue does not reach out to you and would make a poor set of Christmas lights. Blue areas can also appear to recede and increase the garden's sense of spaciousness and mystery. It is attributes such as these that make the subtlety of this colour something of a virtue.

When associating blues consider the effect of the background colours and the dominant lighting because blues look very different as light conditions alter. In damp countries blue is inseparable from green and they hold hands all the time. Their natural closeness in the spectrum means that they literally reinforce one another. Though blue and yellow arrangements are popular the contrast of tone makes them pretty rather than richly dramatic. You can achieve a richer unity with gentian *Anchusa azurea* 'Loddon Royalist' emerging from a mass of green summer foliage combined with other intense blues such as *Delphinium belladonna* 'Lamartine', *Salvia* x *sylvestris* 'May Night' and violet-blue *Campanula glomerata* 'Superba'. A similar effect can be created in semi-shade using deep blue *Aconitum carmichaelii* 'Arendsii'. The blue flower tones so well with the dark foliage that a black-and-white photograph would not distinguish between the two. By these means the blues are enriched.

Mid-blues and powder blues add vitality to a planting. *Campanula lactiflora* 'Prichard's Variety' has lavender-blue flowers in midsummer while prickly *Echinops bannaticus* 'Taplow Blue', *Eryngium* x *oliverianum* with its steel-blue bracts and blue-stemmed *E. bourgatii* with its azure

teasle-like flowers add textural contrast and some of the blue aquilegias may still be around. Irises such as inky *Iris* 'Black Swan' or paler *I.* 'Jane Phillips' flirt for a while and then leave behind glaucous sword-like leaves. They add pattern and blend in with the azure scheme. If the soil is reasonably moist opt for the delicate blue flowers and lush, reedy leaves of *Iris sibirica*. Tall early-flowering *Geranium* x *magnificum*, pale blue *G. pratense* 'Mrs. Kendall Clark' and the reliable

Above
Agave parryi huachucensis is intensely blue.
Top near right
Lilac, mauve and purple *Galega orientalis*,
***Campanula persicifolia*, *Delphinium* 'Faust',**
***Geranium* 'Brookside' and *Viola cornuta*.**
Top far right
The glaucous foliage of these aquilegias echoes the
colour of the euphorbia.
Bottom near right
Massed aquilegias with *Nepeta* 'Six Hills Giant'.
Bottom far right
Lilac-flowered *Buddleja davidii* 'Nanho Blue'
planted above *Echinops ritro* 'Veitch's Blue'.

G. 'Johnson's Blue' that masses at about 30 cm (1 ft) accommodate easily to most soils. For the late show paler blues are provided by perovskias and caryopteris with structured agapanthus as well as the startling bright blue colour of the hardy *Ceratostigma willmottianum* with its reddening autumn leaves.

Other flower colours will enhance the blues as long as they are not strident. Fluffy cream *Thalictrum aquilegiifolium album* and the palest cream *Achillea* 'Moonshine' deal kindly with the blues in a way that I find lacking with the yellows. A few whitened blues will also flatter gently including powder-blue *Veronica gentianoides* and *Phlox paniculata* 'Blue Ice' whose pure white flowers are washed with pale blue. Subtly different is the small, blueish white *Geranium renardii* which has china-white flowers and dark green, velvet leaves and the luminous white *Geranium sylvaticum* 'Album' with light green foliage.

I like to complement these plants with greys. The steely *Phormium tenax* or pewter-coloured *Macleaya cordata* as well as silver *Artemisia absinthium* 'Lambrook Silver' and furry *Stachys byzantina* add lightness. These silver leaves seem to shimmer with the fine white hairs on the surface catching the light. Some foliage plants also have blueish tones. For example, there is a wealth of hostas whose leaves have a waxy coating that affects their colour. *Hosta sieboldiana* has blue, overlapping leaves and the compact *H.* 'Halcyon' is even bluer. Provided that the conditions are not too dry they could be part of a blue association. Otherwise there is no leaf bluer than *Ruta graveolens*. Alternatively, in hotter climates you might exploit the blue tones of cacti or pale blue, fleshy leaves of *Sedum* 'Herbstfreude'.

A Blue-Purple Border Beautiful as this border is, it is important to gain an understanding of the horticultural needs of all the plants that have been selected. They all enjoy the border's south-facing aspect as well as the very dry, slightly acidic and stony soil. Although this garden is actually in England it contains many plants that we would normally associate with the Mediter-ranean. The border is also banked which means that the soil has to be retained by a series of horizontal logs. The sloping site has the effect of focusing the heat and ensures the good drainage that is vital for the chosen plants. As a further insurance before planting, the owners also incorporated quantities of gravel into the soil in order to maintain its free-draining charac-

Spring

KEY *(H = Height; S = Spread)*

Spring-Flowering Plants
1. *Tulipa* 'Bleu Aimable', *H: 55 cm (22 in)*
2. *Tulipa marjolletti, H: 50 cm (20 in)*
3. *Crocus etruscus* 'Zwanenberg',
H: 10 cm (4 in); S: 3-8 cm (1¼-3 in)
4. *Tulipa* 'Ballade', *H: 50 cm (20 in)*
5. *Muscari armeniacum, H: 15-20 cm*
(6-8 in); S: 8-10 cm (3-4 in)
6. *Brunnera macrophylla, H: 45 cm (1½ ft); S:*
60 cm (2 ft)
7. *Brunnera macrophylla* 'Hadspen Cream',
H: 45 cm (1½ ft); S: 60 cm (2 ft)
8. *Omphalodes verna, H and S: 20 cm (8 in)*
9. *Symphytum ibericum, H: 25 cm (10 in);*
S: 60 cm (2 ft)
10. *Symphytum* 'Hidcote Blue', *H: 50 cm*
(20 in); S: 60 cm (2 ft)
11. *Narcissus* 'Jenny', *H: 30 cm (1 ft)*
12. *Bergenia* 'Silberlicht', *H: 30 cm (1 ft);*
S: 50 cm (20 in)
13. *Heliotropium peruvianum,*
H and S: 60 cm (2 ft)
14. *Euphorbia myrsinites, H: 5-8 cm (2-3 in);*
S: 20 cm (8 in)

Spring Plan

Spring, above Much of the colour in spring comes from bulbs planted in the previous autumn. *Muscari armeniacum* provides intensely blue flower spikes among pale blue comfrey (*Symphytum* 'Hidcote Blue') to establish the blue notes of the border. The bearded *Iris* 'Blue Denim', purple *Tulipa* 'Ballade' and purple-blue *Crocus etruscus* 'Zwanenberg' also make an appearance.

ter. As a result, the plants in the border never have their roots miserably sitting in the wet, even during a continuously wet season.

The design of this border is based on a restricted colour palette of soothing blues and purples. The background of deep green rhododendron foliage serves to intensify the blueness although other carefully selected

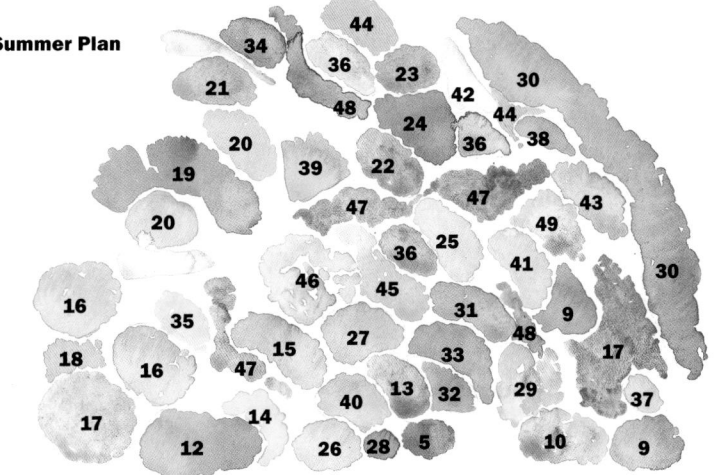

Summer-Flowering Plants

15. *Iris* 'Blue Denim', *H: 25 cm (10 in);*
S: indefinite

16. *Iris pallida* 'Aurea Variegata',
H: 70-100 cm (28-39 in); S: indefinite

17. *Nepeta* 'Six Hills Giant',
H and S: 60 cm (2 ft)

18. *Helianthemum* 'Wisley Pink',
H and : 30 cm (1 ft)

19. *Iris germanica, H: 60-120 cm (2-4 ft);*
S: indefinite

20. *Helianthemum* 'White Queen',
H and S: 30 cm (1 ft)

21. *Salvia officinalis* 'Aurea', *H: 60 cm (2 ft);*
S: 90 cm (3 ft)

22. *Salvia officinalis* Purpurascens Group,
H: 60 cm (2 ft); S: 90 cm (3 ft)

23. *Ruta graveolens* 'Jackman's Blue',
H: 60-90 cm (2-3 ft)

24. *Rosa* 'Nevada', *H and S: 2.2 m (7 ft)*

25. *Artemisia schmidtiana* 'Nana',
H: 8-30 cm (3-12 in); S: 60 cm (2 ft)

26. *Thymus vulgaris* 'Silver Posie',
H and S: 30 cm (1 ft)

27. *Cistus x hybridus, H and S: 90cm (3ft)*

28. *Meconopsis cambrica, H: 30-45 cm*
(1-1½ ft); S: 30 cm (1 ft)

29. *Anisodonetea capensis, H: 90 cm (3 ft);*
S: 60 cm (2 ft)

30. *Rhododendron ponticum,*
H and S: 2.5 m (8 ft)

31. *Salvia officinalis, H: 60 cm (2 ft);*
S: 90 cm (3 ft)

32. *Festuca glauca, H and S: 10 cm (4 in)*

33. *Salvia microphylla microphylla,*
H and S: 1.2 m (4 ft)

34. *Santolina rosmarinifolia*
rosmarinifolia, H: 60 cm (2 ft); S: 90 cm (3 ft)

35. *Achillea millefolium* 'Cerise Queen',
H: 60 cm (2 ft); S: 20 cm (8 in)

36. *Lavandula angustifolia* 'Munstead',
H and S: 75 cm (2½ ft)

37. *Erysimum* 'Janet's Brick Red',
H and S: 30 cm (1 ft)

38. *Persicaria bistorta* 'Superba',
H: 60-75 cm (2-2½ ft); S: 60 cm (2 ft)

39. *Libertia formosa, H: 70 cm (28 in);*
S: 20 cm (8 in)

40. *Helianthemum* 'Wisley Primrose',
H: 23 cm (9 in); S: 30 cm (1 ft)

41. *Thymus* 'Porlock', *H: 8 cm (3 in);*
S: 20 cm (8 in)

42. *Chamaecytisus albus, H: 30 cm (1 ft);*
S: 90 cm (3 ft)

43. *Foeniculum vulgare* 'Purpureum',
H: 1.8 m (6 ft); S: 45 cm (1½ ft)

44. *Digitalis purpurea, H: 90-150 cm (3-5 ft);*
S: 60 cm (2 ft)

45. *Verbascum phoeniceum* (pink),
H: 75 cm (2½ ft); S: 60 cm (2 ft)

46. *Verbascum phoeniceum*
(white), *H: 75 cm (2½ ft); S: 60 cm (2 ft)*

47. *Allium cristophii, H: 15-40 cm (6-16 in); S: 15-20 cm (6-8 in)*

48. *Nectaroscordum siculum,*
H: 1.2 m (4 ft); S: 30-45 cm (1-1½ ft)

49. *Perovskia* 'Blue Spire', *H: 90-120 cm (3-4 ft); S: 90 cm (3 ft)*

Summer Plan

Summer, above In addition to the main mid-summer blues of the border from *Lavandula angustifolia* 'Munstead' and blue *Nepeta* 'Six Hills Giant', the blue-purple colour scheme is intensified further by purples, lilacs and magenta-crimsons that are closely associated in the colour spectrum. These include the upright purple allium flowers, the pinkish-purple foxgloves, the colourful *Erysimum*, the purple sage (*Salvia officinalis* Purpurascens Group), the small *Achillea millefolium* 'Cerise Queen' and the tender evergreen *Heliotropium arborescens*. This shrub has purple flowers from late spring through to the winter. Wines, crimsons and cool pinks also blend in with *Helianthemum* 'Wisley Pink' and the magenta-coloured flowers of *Anisodontea capensis*. The pink and white flowers of *Verbascum phoeniceum*, the delicate cream umbels of *Nectaroscordum siculum* and the startlingly white flowers of *Cistus* x *hybridus* (*C.* x *corbariensis*) all serve to lighten the overall colour scheme.

plants provide some further colour contrasts. The addition of cream and white flowers such as helianthemums and verbascums also create other centres of interest in the border as the seasons pass.

Much of the chosen foliage is silver and grey in colour. This includes the evergreen artemisias, thymes and lavenders that lighten the overall effect of the border and complement the colour scheme. These plants also create an image that is redolent of the Mediterranean. *Artemisia schmidtiana* is a semi-evergreen perennial with deeply cut, silver leaves while *Lavandula angustifolia* 'Munstead' has narrow, aromatic leaves and tiny, fragrant, blue flowers. Both early and late in the year bulbs are an invaluable means of introducing colour and can be worked in among the perennials to extend the flowering season. So, tulips, muscari and narcissus provide the

Late Summer/Early Autumn

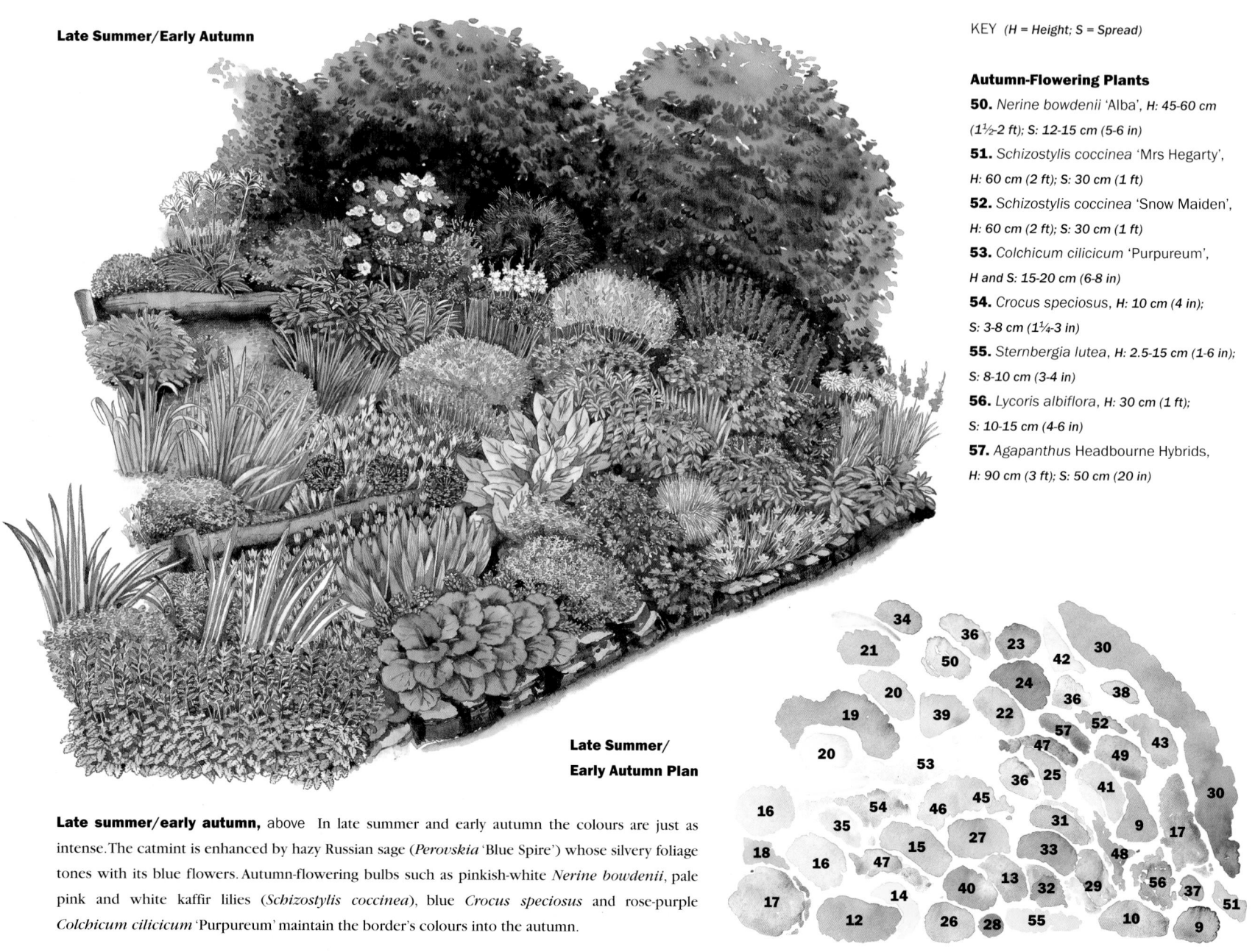

KEY *(H = Height; S = Spread)*

Autumn-Flowering Plants

50. *Nerine bowdenii* 'Alba', *H: 45-60 cm (1½-2 ft); S: 12-15 cm (5-6 in)*

51. *Schizostylis coccinea* 'Mrs Hegarty', *H: 60 cm (2 ft); S: 30 cm (1 ft)*

52. *Schizostylis coccinea* 'Snow Maiden', *H: 60 cm (2 ft); S: 30 cm (1 ft)*

53. *Colchicum cilicicum* 'Purpureum', *H and S: 15-20 cm (6-8 in)*

54. *Crocus speciosus, H: 10 cm (4 in); S: 3-8 cm (1¼-3 in)*

55. *Sternbergia lutea, H: 2.5-15 cm (1-6 in); S: 8-10 cm (3-4 in)*

56. *Lycoris albiflora, H: 30 cm (1 ft); S: 10-15 cm (4-6 in)*

57. *Agapanthus* Headbourne Hybrids, *H: 90 cm (3 ft); S: 50 cm (20 in)*

Late Summer/ Early Autumn Plan

Late summer/early autumn, above In late summer and early autumn the colours are just as intense. The catmint is enhanced by hazy Russian sage (*Perovskia* 'Blue Spire') whose silvery foliage tones with its blue flowers. Autumn-flowering bulbs such as pinkish-white *Nerine bowdenii*, pale pink and white kaffir lilies (*Schizostylis coccinea*), blue *Crocus speciosus* and rose-purple *Colchicum cilicicum* 'Purpureum' maintain the border's colours into the autumn.

displays of colour in the spring while the colchicums, the autumn-flowering crocus, the sternbergias and the nerines maintain the colour scheme until the autumn.

In late summer, the border also contains *Lycoris albiflora*. This is a rather unusual bulb that has ivory-coloured flowers emerging from a leafless base. The leaves develop later on and will last until the following spring. Other plants that are at their best now include the light blue *Agapanthus* Headbourne Hybrids. In autumn appears blue-flowered *Crocus speciosus* with grass-like foliage and rose-purple *Colchicum cilicicum* 'Purpureum'. A rather good contrast is provided by *Nerine bowdenii* 'Alba' which has white flowers with pinkish overtones.

Right

The border is shown here in the early summer, a time of the year which celebrates the colour scheme in all its intensity. The powerfully blue colour of the *Iris* 'Blue Denim' and Russian sage (*Perovskia*) are enhanced by the rounded, purple flower heads of *Allium cristophii* as well as by white and pink *Verbascum phoeniceum*. These summer-flowering perennials bring a splash of brighter colour to the bed. The tall, pinkish-white flowers of *Persicaria bistorta* 'Superba' are flattered at the back of the bed by the hazy foliage of bronze fennel (*Foeniculum vulgare* 'Purpureum').

CLASSIC COLOUR COMBINATIONS

Traditions have developed in the gardening world that certain colours go well with one another which has led to classic combinations. So silver foliage is often used with pinks, pale blues, creams and clarets while 'hot' colour schemes use only permutations of red, orange and yellow with green foliage.

A Hot Border The richness of a hot border depends on selecting plants with the most saturated colours that are in close proximity in the colour spectrum. There is no room for pastels and only a very few silver-greys. The

should be planted in large bold masses. You could also add some scarlet *Crocosmia* 'Lucifer' at 90 cm (3 ft) tall. This plant will create a dense thicket of sword-like leaves that can resist both wind and rain. Further brilliance might come from *Monarda* 'Cambridge Scarlet', *Lychnis chalcedonica* and *Kniphofia rooperi* as well as lily-flowered *Hemerocallis* 'Stafford' with its grassy foliage, deep red lupins for their vertical rhythms and *Heuchera* 'Red Spangles' with its mass of tiny, deep red flowers. *Oenothera fruticosa* 'Fireworks' could be allowed to distribute itself randomly because, despite its name, the flowers have a cooling effect although there are red hints in the

relationships are intense and furthered by using plum-, purple- or brown-coloured foliage as part of the scheme rather than the glaucous greens. Yellow, orange and red are really the most important colours although any mix of these is valuable.

The yellows should be golden rather like *Ligularia przewalskii* or the magnificent 2 m (6½ ft) tall *Inula magnifica* whose flowers resemble flamboyant ostrich feathers. Such a plant will set the pace. Picking up the gauntlet comes *Heliopsis helianthoides scabra* which has rounded, densely petalled, slightly more orange-toned flowers and grows up to 1.2 m (4 ft) tall. Both

Above left
Primary red *Monarda* 'Cambridge Scarlet' and yellow *Dahlia* 'Bednall Beauty' look dramatic in association with *Ligularia* 'The Rocket' and *Calceolaria* 'Kentish Hero'. Brown *Carex* grass soothes the colour scheme.
Above centre
A hot border in which red *Dahlia* 'Bishop of Llandaff', allied to red *Atriplex hortensis rubra* and *Penstemon* 'Garnet', dominates yellow rudbeckias.
Above right
Early in the year these lovely red tulips form a striking horizontal layer above a line of golden-flowered *Erysimum* which are edged very neatly by a row of deep blue forget-me-nots (*Myosotis*).

plant. In short, red and yellow associations are fiery but they are at their most effective when the dominant colour is red while the hot yellows should be worked in with a little more discretion. A little 'creative' weeding is easily done when necessary.

Among the reds and yellows some oranges will fuel the flames. The familiar cone-shaped flowers of *Rudbeckia hirta* are a tawny orange colour while *Hemerocallis* 'Burning Daylight' is an intense mahogany orange. Add a dash of red-brown *Alstroemeria psittacina* and layers of *Achillea* 'The Beacon' to enhance the patterns in the scheme. This planting association is also suited to attractive *Iris germanica* forms with old-gold, burnt-orange and mahogany-brown colouring that leave behind grey-green leaves once the flowers have departed. Later on bronze-coloured *Helenium* 'Moerheim Beauty' and *Dahlia* 'Bishop of Llandaff' might be added to reassert the vermilion colour.

You can add other more luscious colours to accentuate the colour relationships through contrast while reaffirming the intensity of the scheme. I suggest threading through deep purple-blue *Aconitum* 'Spark's Variety' and *Eryngium* x *oliverianum* with its metallic blueness and spiky form. This will not be too intense if you also include some densely packed greens and

Above left
Dark red *Plantago* leaves merge beautifully with bright red nasturtiums. Also part of the planting scheme are red dahlias and astrantias.

Above centre
Here vivid red dahlias, nicotianas and crimson-red roses surround the tall, stately flower spikes of yellow *Kniphofia* 'Goldelse' which help to lighten the overall effect of this red-oriented colour scheme.

Above right
The scarlet, orange and chrome hues of *Helenium* 'Butterpat', *Dahlia* 'Tally-ho' and *Achillea* 'Coronation Gold' have been successfully combined with the fiery orange flowers of crocosmia to create a powerfully 'hot' border.

browns. All the above plants have green foliage that stirs up the complementary effects but the dark brown-leaved elder *Sambucus nigra* 'Guincho Purple', sited behind and overseeing the other plants, will settle the group. You could also include massed *Rosa moyesii* 'Geranium', which has fresh, green, fern-like foliage dotted with brilliant, flagon-shaped hips and the modern hybrid *Rosa* 'Scarlet Fire' with similarly brick-red hips. The foliage among these plants should be distinctive so you could also include a large, red-leaved *Berberis thunbergii atropurpurea*, a few brown-leaved *Viburnum sargentii* 'Onondaga', grey *Phormium tenax* and some hazy bronze fennel.

A Cool Border Cooler colour schemes, using pale blues, pinks, lavenders, mauves, lemons and creams, can be used within a large space containing mixed shrubs and perennials or within a shaded spot. Alternatively, these colours would suit a hot, gravel-covered bed to create a mass of shapes and textures at ground level. If you have room, you might add stronger colours to compensate for the inevitable fade-out of light at midday.

Evergreens such as escallonias, *Carpenteria californica*, with its dark leaves and white flowers, and *Garrya elliptica* provide a dark, structural background for these colours. In sheltered sites silver-leaved *Pyrus salicifolia* 'Pendula' and varieties of *Pittosporum tenuifolium* offer pale and variegated colours. Among the deciduous shrubs include white-flowered *Rhodotypos scandens* with its textured leaves and the wide-spreading *Stachyurus praecox* that flowers in late winter. Rounded shrubs such as pale *Potentilla fruticosa* 'Primrose Beauty' could also be considered.

The leaf colour in a cool border can come from silver artemisias, santolinas, stachys and lavenders. Flowers should be the paler versions of their genus including cream, daisy-flowered *Achillea* 'Anthea', the pale yellow flower spikes of *Verbascum chaixii* 'Gainsborough' and primrose-yellow X *Solidaster luteus* 'Lemore'. Campanulas, scabious and agapanthus all have pale

blue forms while *Anchusa azurea* 'Opal' is an unexpectedly light blue. There are also a variety of pink flowers to choose from including mallows (*Malva*), sidalceas and carnations as well as pink forms of geranium, astilbe, monarda and foxtail lily (*Eremurus*). Many blueish plants, such as thalictrums, lavender, cardamine and violas, also veer towards lilac. The tall, pale purple *Verbena bonariensis* can weave its way through larger herbaceous flowers while violet-tinged *Acanthus spinosus* might provide static, architectural form within the groups. You could also consider the range of cool colours supplied by delphiniums, lupins, day lilies, geraniums and hybrid irises.

For shaded sites, particularly with damp soil, luminous blues and whites are ideal, revelling so much in the reduced light that the colours seem to glow. For example, the 6 m (20 ft) tall white-flowered lily-of-the-valley tree (*Clethra arborea*) and the smaller 3 m (10 ft) pink, acid-loving calico bush (*Kalmia latifolia*) are both suited to light shade. Cool pink, lavender and white rhododendrons also need acidic conditions. The tree peony *Paeonia suffruticosa* 'Rock's Variety' will also do well given a little more light. These shrubs should be planted with white foxgloves, pink and white *Anemone* x *hybrida* forms and the cream-flowered *Smilacena racemosa* as well as ferns and paler astilbes whose colours look stronger in shade. Always be sure to check if shade-loving plants are ericaceous and add some bulbs such as snowdrops, leucojums, *Lilium martagon* and *Camassia leitchlinii*.

If you have a sunny garden then the choice of plants is quite different. You can opt for a more open, low-level style of planting using hardier, smaller rock plants, dwarf shrubs such as *Cistus*

'Silver Pink' with grey leaves and light pink flowers and the evergreen X *Halimiocistus sahuccii* whose dark leaves set off pure white flowers. The small, glossy, blue-flowered evergreen *Ceanothus thyrsiflorus repens*, lavenders, santolinas and *Convolvulus cneorum* are also suitable. You might also want to work in some pale pink, white or blue daphnes or *Parahebe catarractae*.

Rock roses such as pale *Helianthemum* 'Wisley Pink' also provide low, flower-covered mounds in the border while many dianthus forms, alpine geraniums, small veronicas, running campanulas and thrifts are pale in colour. Some finely formed, slightly taller plants such as pale blue *Linum perenne*, blue, pink or white aquilegias or even grasses such as pale-flowered *Pennisetum orientale* or the smaller form of fluffy *Stipa tenuissima* add texture to the pale-toned flowers.

Roses also come in a wide range of cool, pastel shades, including soft pinks, pale yellows and rich creams. They prefer an open, sunny site and moist but well-drained soil. Whether you choose shrub roses or climbing roses you can create a strikingly cool border with these plants, particularly when you underplant them with low-growing flowers with the same cool-toned colours such as lavenders, blue-flowered rue (*Ruta graveolens*) and softly grey or purple sage (*Salvia officinalis* Purpurascens Group).

Top right
The flowers of *Rosa* 'Bonica' and *Penstemon* 'Hidcote Pink' are an almost identical pink. They are set off here by dark *Clematis* 'Etoile Violette' and the grey-purple foliage of *Rosa glauca*.
Right
White delphiniums, *Argyranthemum* 'Jamaica Primrose', cream *Scabiosa columbria ochroleuca* and lemon lupins are used here in a pastel border.

Right

Cerise and purple blend together beautifully as is seen when *Salvia* x *superba* is planted in front of hollyhocks (*Alcea rosea*), *Dahlia* 'Rutland Water' and dots of *Knautia macedonica*.

Below

A pergola has been covered with a variety of different climbing roses including wine-red *Rosa* 'Bleu Magenta', cool pink *R.* 'Bantry Bay' and the lovely white *R.* 'Wedding Day'. The roses have been underplanted with pastel-blue nepeta.

Near right

Tulipa 'Queen of Night' is a particularly striking, spring-flowering bulb because of the intensity of its near-black colour. This contrasts with *T.* 'Magier' and the sea of *Myosotis* 'Blue Ball' and purple violas in which the tulips are planted.

Far right

Strong fuchsia-pink *Gladiolus communis byzantinus* creates a striking association with *Iris* 'Wild Echo', wine-coloured *Cirsium rivulare* 'Atropurpureum' and self-sown *Lunaria annua*.

Wine-Red, Purple, Mid-Blue and Green Playing with colours is part of the joy of gardening and it is enjoyable to explore a range of different colour effects. Using colours of the same shade or tone such as this wine-red, purple, mid-blue and green combination can create dramatically rich results.

Where possible, establish a dark background of purple-red leaves such as *Cotinus coggygria* 'Rubrifolius Group'. This could be planted next to a tall *Viburnum rhytidophyllum* with its coarse, mid-green leaves to provide a textural contrast without competing with the tonal colour range. Tall buddlejas like *Buddleja davidii* 'Black Knight' or *B. d.* 'Royal Red' add purple or maroon-

Climbers such as *Clematis* 'Rouge Cardinal', *C.* 'Niobe', *C. viticella*, intensely blue *C.* 'Polish Spirit' and purple-leaved climber *Vitis vinifera* 'Purpurea' add height as well as colour. These shrubs and climbers provide the foundation for attractive perennial associations. Four 'true-blue' perennials work well in this scheme including *Anchusa azurea* 'Royal Blue', *Aconitum* 'Spark's Variety', *Agapanthus* 'Bressingham Blue' and *Salvia* x *sylvestris* 'May Night'. You can then add reddish-violet *Lythrum salicaria* 'Firecandle' and *Sidalcea* 'Croftway Red' with *Phlox paniculata* 'Vintage Wine' to reinforce the purple theme and dots of wine-red *Knautia macedonica*.

red flower spikes. The blue hollies such as *Ilex* x *meserveae* 'Blue Princess' are also dark green but their glossy leaves reflect distinctly blue tones. Early in the season, the rich blue colour of forget-me-nots (*Myosotis*) are invaluable in a border devoted to this colour sheme, particularly in association with deep purple varieties of tulip. In the summer, the dark green foliage and cerise flowers of *Cistus* x *pulverulentus* could also be included as long as it is sited further forward to catch more sun. For much of the year the mid-green leaves of another useful shrub, *Clerodendrum trichotomum fargesii*, are neutral but by late summer it has extraordinarily blue berries surrounded by a ruff of wine-red calyces. Another late season shrub is *Callicarpa bodinieri* 'Profusion' with its amazingly chemical-coloured, purple fruits.

Hybrid delphiniums also come in a range of purples, lilacs and deep blues that the painter would envy while the magenta *Geranium psilostemon* can electrify the picture. You might like to include paler blues such as blue-violet *Salvia sclarea turkestanica* and mid-blue centaureas. Later in the season, blue and purple asters such as *Aster novi-belgii* 'Carnival' could be punctuated with purple alliums, *Liriope muscari* or lavenders.

Light greens, such as *Helleborus foetidus* early in the year, would be striking in this scheme. Later the green flower spikes of *Kniphofia* 'Green Jade' and the fluffy, green flowers of *Heuchera* 'Green Ivory' are ideal. I would also consider greenish-white *Astrantia major* interplanted with maroon-leaved *Ajuga reptans* 'Burgundy Glow' as a ground cover.

UNUSUAL COLOUR COMBINATIONS

Just as ideas on combining colour were revolutionized by painters such as Matisse so gardeners are starting to experiment with colour schemes. Using unusual colours such as black, brown, purple, lime-green or maroon produces remarkably stylish effects.

Burnt Orange, Rust-Red, Lime-Green and Deep Purple The purples and greens just described look quite different associated with hot tones instead of cool ones. Oranges and rust-reds have a 'complementary' relationship with purples that is very powerful. For example, delphiniums come in a range of purples including the black-eyed, deep purple *Delphinium* 'Finsteraarhorn' and the dark purple *D.* 'Purple Triumph'. The smaller belladonna hybrid, *D. bellandonna* 'Völkerfriden', is an equally intense gentian-purple colour.

Such powerful plants should sit with a mass of bright orange *Crocosmia* 'Lucifer' to create vivid contrast. To settle the matter the large, copper-purple shrub *Corylus maxima* 'Purpurea' would provide a substantial backcloth. The purple-tinted Boston ivy (*Parthenocissus tricuspidata*) flares up in the autumn and in summer the scarlet-orange flowers of trumpet vine (*Campsis radicans*) add vitality.

Other plants can heat up the purples. Early in the year *Euphorbia griffithii* 'Fireglow' adds more orange to the border. By early summer hybrid irises, such as the tall, bearded, brown *Iris* 'Autumn Leaves', provide shades of bronze and chestnut-brown. In high summer, tiger lilies (*Lilium lancifolium*) light up a border and by midsummer the hardy daylilies provide the same cinnamon-bronzes as the irises as well as coppers and Indian reds.

You can increase the brightness with *Phormium* 'Sundowner', *P.* 'Apricot Queen' and also the smaller *P.* 'Bronze Baby', which echo the orange-red hues.

You could also add scarlet-peach *Achillea* 'Fanal' and *A. millefolium* 'Paprika'. Brightly coloured *Rudbeckia hirta* 'Marmalade' speaks for itself while brilliant red *Astilbe* 'Fanal' and *A.* 'Granat' are ideal for damp soil. The yellow-orange combination could be echoed with the flowers of *Verbascum chaixii* 'Cotswold Queen'.

Later in the year, the vivid, burnt-orange colours of the sneezeweeds (*Helenium*) might be introduced. Their colours would be enhanced by the violet-blue flowers of a Californian lilac such as *Ceanothus* 'Delight' and deep blue *Ceratostigma willmottianum*. The tawny orange *Phygelius capensis* 'Winchester Fanfare' appears at the same time. Red-hot pokers such as bronze-flowered *Kniphofia galpinii* and deep scarlet *K.* 'Samuel's Sensation' offer the same range.

There are also green-spiked cultivars such as *K.* 'Green Jade' to challenge the rusts, scarlet-oranges and purples. *Alchemilla mollis* has pastel-green foliage and lime-green flowers while the half-hardy *Nicotiana langsdorfii* has lime-green bell flowers as does the pretty *Molucella laevis*.

Top Row
Left **This rich-red *Crocosmia* 'Lucifer' is aptly named.** Middle **Red and gold daylilies (*Hemerocallis*) look striking planted with lime-yellow *Solidago* 'Mimosa'.** Right **The fanned, orange leaves of *Libertia peregrinans* seem to glow among purple *Muscari botryoides*.**
Middle Row
Left **Blue *Polemonium* and burnt-orange *Alstroemeria* have been backed by lime-green *Philadelphus coronarius* 'Aureus'.** Middle **Purple *Anchusa* provides an attractive backdrop for hot orange dahlias.** Right **Plum-coloured *Astrantia major* 'Claret' intensifies the impact of this blue *Clematis* x *eriostemon*.**
Bottom Row
Left **A classic combination of forget-me-nots (*Myosotis*) with orange tulips.** Middle **These orange marigolds make vivid partners for bronze-red aquilegias.** Right **Magenta ornamental cabbages blaze among yellow marigolds and eschscholzias.**

Chocolate, Purple and Lemon Extreme shades of darkness such as chocolate or purple can be used to create contrast or to enliven a plant mass. The framework provided by dark foliaged plants such as deep purple elder *Sambucus nigra* 'Guincho Purple', the dark bronzes of *Corylus maxima* 'Purpurea' and *Fagus sylvatica* 'Purpurea Pendula' are ideal. I would also include dusty, dark red *Cotinus coggygria* 'Royal Purple' and the blackened overtones of red *Berberis thunbergii atropurpurea* if there is light shining directly on the front of the border. Any of these shrubs will flatter pale-toned leaves or lemon-yellow flowers.

Among dark flower colours there is nothing so dominant as *Veratrum nigrum*. This is a magnificent plant that has deep reddish-chocolate flower spikes above lush, pleated leaves. A horticultural challenge, it needs a moist site in sun or part-shade. The 1.8 m (6 ft) tall *Cimicifuga simplex* 'Brunette' also prefers damp conditions and light shade. The white flowers come late in summer and emerge from large, bronze-black leaves. Easier to grow, even in dry shade, is the mourning widow (*Geranium phaeum*) with its small, purple-black flowers above slender stems. As always you can look among the selection of hybrid irises and daylilies (*Hemerocallis*) when you are searching

Sometimes the contradiction of opposites creates harmony, a sort of yin-yang balance. In this way dark flower colours among luminously pale foliage such as artemisias and pastel-toned flowers can add definition to an indefinite grouping. The hardy annual dark red-purple orach (*Atriplex hortensis rubra*) is often seeded into soft grey borders for this reason. This pale, sophisticated scheme is maybe just too restrained for some and a hint of darkness may revitalize it. Consider then the effect of a mass of *Delphinium* Black Night Group among 90 cm (3 ft) tall *Achillea* 'Moonshine' or alternatively the 60 cm (2 ft) perennial chocolate *Cosmos atrosanguineus*.

Above left
Simple cerise flowers of *Geranium* 'Patricia' have been successfully combined with flat-headed, primrose-yellow flowers of *Achillea* 'Martina' to make a particularly intense partnership.

Above centre
***Geranium psilostemon* has strong magenta flowers with black eyes and is strikingly accompanied here by cream achilleas.**

Above right
Pale pink *Monarda* 'Cherokee' with their chocolate-coloured centres are seen here in association with *Artemisia* 'Jim Russell' and the intensely wine-red flowers of *Atriplex hortensis rubra*.

for the specific colours for this planting scheme. For example, the brown *Iris* 'Dusky Challenger', *I.* 'Brown Trout', *I.* 'Brownstone' and *I.* 'Bronze Cloud' are, as their names suggest, particularly good choices. In addition, there are also some beautifully dark-toned, purple-red daylilies such as the deep maroon *Hemerocallis* 'Black Magic'. These will all lend a rather sultry charm to the colour scheme.

When it comes to choosing the yellow to associate with these dark hues of chocolate-brown and purple you should select the cool-toned, pale yellows that provide a far softer contrast of colour than their sharp, canary-yellow colleagues. Fortunately, many yellow-flowering plants have forms in this cool colour range. These include the 45 cm (1½ ft) tall *Coreopsis verticillata* 'Moonbeam' and the tall, branching *Verbascum chaixii* 'Gainsborough' whose pale yellow flower spikes reach up to just under 1.5 m (5 ft) above woolly grey leaves. You could also include a 1.2 m (4 ft) tall *Cephalaria gigantea*. This yellow scabious has pincushion heads of primrose-yellow flowers in early summer. Another good choice would be the lemon-coloured, daisy-flowered *Anthemis tinctoria* 'E.C. Buxton' as well as the thrusting flower spikes of *Kniphofia* 'Little Maid' that have the added attraction of

Above left
This magical contrast of colours late in the year is provided by the bronze leaves of *Heuchera* 'Palace Purple' beside silvery, lacy *Artemisia* 'Powis Castle' and *Aster amellus* 'Pink Zenith'.

Above centre
Mahogany-coloured *Iris* 'Kent Pride' look beautiful set in a sea of purple-leaved *Heuchera* 'Rachel' while *Erysimum* 'Bowles' Mauve' is a suitable companion.

Above right
This triumphant colour association based on vegetables in a decorative potager includes red drumhead cabbages, lollo rosso lettuce, bronze fennel, flowering chives and the dense, green leaves of parsley.

gradually whitening as they reach maturity. Again the ever versatile daylilies have pale yellow varieties in their repertoire such as *Hemerocallis* 'Classy Lassie'. You may also consider adding *Achillea* 'Taygetea' with its flat heads of lemon-yellow flowers or *A.* 'Moonshine' that has bright yellow flowers throughout the summer. If you would like to incorporate some coloured foliage plants as well as this mass of flowers, you may consider adding *Milium effusum* 'Aureum'. This is a very pretty, delicate, buff-yellow grass that will seed itself randomly but unthreateningly. It will, of course, also sway gently in the breeze, bringing movement as well as colour to these companions.

Fairground Colour You may in fact dislike the colour schemes suggested so far because you are reluctant to restrict colour in the garden. Using all the colours of the spectrum may be far more appealing. Does this mean you simply find a space and plant what comes to hand? We have all done this but I nearly always regret it because the results can be disappointing, even with desirable plants. So what should you do?

When summer arrives so does the colour. The phrase 'a riot of colour' is often used and this puzzles me. Surely we prefer drama, beauty or tranquillity? Perhaps what we really mean by this expression is a celebration of colour. To feast ourselves with colour so that the plants look 'right' we need to understand the scene we are setting. Creating a fairground border is not simply a question of using the primary hues of red, yellow and blue against a green background. There are deep purple-blues, powder-pale blues, rust reds and wine reds, peaches and pinks, primrose and lemon yellows as well as a multitude of neutral greens. Select the colours for their tonal relationships, whether dark or pale, to achieve a brilliant effect. You can find varieties offering colour values among the daylilies, irises, geraniums, salvias, delphiniums,

Top far left
This informal planting is filled with flowers of varying shades of pink and orange including pink *Ranunculus*, *Nemesia* and *Heuchera* 'Rachel'.
Top near left
Bicoloured toadflax (*Linaria maroccana*) provides a fairground mixture from which rise brightly coloured forms of *Ranunculus* and *Nemesia*.
Left
A 'dolly mixture' combination of hybrid tulips, mixed double daisies (*Bellis perennis*) and forget-me-nots (*Myosotis*) supply colours as rich as oil paints.
Above right
Alliums mixed with, among others, *Penstemon* 'Garnet' and campanulas create a garden awash with colour.

FAIRGROUND COLOUR

EARLY TO MIDSUMMER:

***Allium hollandicum* 'Purple Sensation'**
Dark purple-rose drumsticks.

***Anchusa azurea* 'Opal'**
Massed pale blue flowers.

***Lupinus* 'The Page'**
Carmine-red tall flower spikes.

Thalictrum aquilegiifolium
Clusters of lilac-pink flowers.

MID- TO LATE SUMMER:

***Achillea filipendulina* 'Gold Plate'**
Rich yellow, flat-headed flowers.

***Aconitum* 'Spark's Variety'**
Deep-violet, hooded flowers.

***Coreopsis verticillata* 'Moonbeam'**
Pale lemon-yellow daisy flowers.

Lychnis chalcedonica
A clump-forming perennial with scarlet flowers.

Potentilla atrosanguinea
Sprays of brilliant red, single flowers.

---

lupins, campanulas, phlox and lilies. There are also a host of ornamental grasses, including green-and-white striped ones, that can also be included in the scheme. You may select pale or deep, hot or cool shades and the colours should be repeated throughout the garden bed or border using the many varieties available in an array of different plant shapes and sizes. These shapes can be rounded, grass-like, layered or spear-like so that the scheme is strikingly attractive and colourful.

If you used different tones of these basic colours the scheme would look completely different as if the garden were bathed in peach-coloured light. Here the bright golds and sunshine-yellows could be warmed by scarlets. Brilliant orange shades could be toned with coppers, and burgundy-purples and marine-blues lightened by apricot, melon and cream. The colour selection is festive with every primary and secondary colour represented. Rudbeckias, dahlias, heleniums, heliopsis, ranunculus, kniphofias, geums, trollius, euphorbias, potentillas, poppies, lychnis, delphiniums, gaillardia and crocosmias provide the colours. Bright and spring-green, bronze and golden-variegated foliage would work in well with the colours repeated back and forth along the bed. Again, the great variety of plant shapes and sizes will sustain the exciting effect of the colour combination, and only a few greys or whites need be included in order to neutralize the image.

I have in fact noticed that cream is an invaluable tone and colour to link with most garden schemes. Unlike white and silver-grey, which can stand out rather strongly, it merges comfortably with hot or cool companions or pale or dark imagery. If you look at traditional fairground painting, you will notice that cream is frequently used, selected instinctively long ago. It worked in the past and it can work for us.

YEAR-ROUND INTEREST

Many contemporary gardens are small spaces, closely interwoven with domestic life which are expected to provide pleasure throughout the year. A framework of enduring evergreens will establish year-round garden structure while the colour of deciduous trees and shrubs in autumn, late-flowering herbaceous plants and early spring bulbs will provide further colour.

Autumn Colour Of the selection of late autumn flowers I favour pink and white hybrid anemones, blue, purple and magenta asters, blue and white agapanthus, yellow-orange coneflowers, spires of cream cimicifuga, stiffly vertical kniphofias and some pink and red persicarias. The huge white daisy flowers of *Leucanthemella serotina* (syn. *Chrysanthemum uliginosum*) are also a triumph of hope against experience while kaffir lilies (*Schizostylis*) continue almost until Christmas, surviving even light frosts. Autumn-flowering crocus and colchicums have pink and purple colouring but I also rather like the butterfly-like flowers of cyclamens. Although autumn flowers bring cheer it is not in the same lush way as summer. So we turn our attention to other matters.

Autumn is special. The sharp air and the bright light simply transforms colours. There is bright orange and gold everywhere and otherwise subtle foliage becomes boldly reddened. For example, the Persian ironwood (*Parrotia persica*) flames widely, sweet gum (*Liquidambar styraciflua*) becomes vermilion and purple, oak trees glow with fiery colour and maples (*Acer*) exceed themselves every year. Wall climbers such as vines and varieties of *Parthenocissus* also flare into life at this time of year.

The other riches of autumn are the decorative fruiting trees and shrubs such as hollies, rowans, cotoneasters, pyracanthas, crab apples and roses that become heavy with red, orange and yellow fruits. Some are splendid soloists like the golden 'crabs' of *Malus* 'Golden Hornet', others appear in dense clusters such as *Sorbus scalaris* and many are distinctive in shape like the flagon-shaped hips of *Rosa moyesii*. There are translucent hips like those of the Guelder rose (*Viburnum opulus*), the pink-flushed berries of *Sorbus vilmorinii*, the pure white fruits of the snowberry (*Symphoricarpus albus*) and the blue fruits of the Oregon grape (*Mahonia aquifolium*).

Increasingly gardeners are not cutting flowerheads back in the autumn because they have seen the effect of frost on *Sedum* 'Herbstfreude' and *Hydrangea arborescens*. There is great beauty in the subtlety of seed-heads such as teasels (*Dipsacus fullonum*), paper-white honesty (*Lunaria annua*) and the delicate *Physalis alkekengi franchetii* while the seeds of many Japanese acers also have a special charm.

Top left
Vivid red *Euonymus alatus apterus* clashes superbly with the crab apples of *Malus* 'Butterball'.
Centre left (above)
Scarlet red-leaved *Berberis thunbergii* 'Silver Beauty' provides a perfect backdrop for the flowers of *Fuchsia magellanica gracilis* 'Variegata'.
Centre left (below)
In late summer these daisy-like asters are flattered by pale pink sedum flowers.
Left
A mop-head hydrangea combined with spiky, grey-green *Euphorbia* is an unusual association.
Right
Claret-red *Acer palmatum* 'Osakazuki' looks magnificent with yellow *Hamamelis mollis*.

Winter Colour The evergreens, for which we should be eternally grateful, make even the most poorly lit winter day bearable. The conifers of the north may have a repetitive presence in thickly snow-clad landscapes but from them come the stalwarts of many gardens whose shapes and textures are richly varied. Among tall trees the main form is the classic narrow vertical (see pages 30-31) although there are also wide-spreading, long-lived cedars.

For larger gardens the weeping, blue-green Brewer's spruce (*Picea breweriana*) with pendulous, trailing branches is a graceful tree. There are few as elegant as this but among the smaller conifers look first for shape and ultimate size such as pencil-slim *Juniperus scopulorum* 'Skyrocket' and weeping, feathery *Chamaecyparis pisifera* 'Filifera Aurea'. There are also wide-spreading, mounding, ground covers such as *J.* x *media* 'Pfitzeriana' and low-growing *J. procumbens* 'Nana'. If you want good texture consider pines (*Pinus*) that come in an exciting variety of shapes and colours like golden, blue, silver, brown and variegated forms. Dense, moss-green conifers such as *Chamaecyparis obtusa* will provide structure all year round.

There are other evergreens to choose from including mahonias, berberis, viburnums and hollies. Some have glossy leaves and are lighter green such as *Choisya ternata* and *Griselinia littoralis*. Variegated shrubs also add colour in winter as do forms of *Elaeagnus* x *ebbingei* and the neat *Euonymus fortunei* 'Silver Queen'. Colour also comes with the dogwoods (*Cornus*) and some shrub willows which have bright red or yellow stems. There are also trees with superb bark including *Prunus serrula* with a mahogany-coloured shine, lime-white *Betula jacquemontii* and red-barked *Arbutus andrachne*. Patterns of form show in winter when Japanese acers display an elegant habit and the twists and turns of *Salix matsudana* 'Tortuosa' are revealed against a grey sky.

Mahonia should also be noted here. *M. japonica* has scented golden racemes and forms of *M.* x *media* such as 'Charity' are deservedly popular for their winter flowers. Other flowers to look for are the tassels of *Garrya*

Above left
Evergreen *Euonymus fortunei* 'Silver Queen' with its distinctive variegated leaves covers the ground in the winter beneath shining, red stems of the dogwood *Cornus alba* 'Sibirica'.
Left
In the stillness created by winter frosts, parchment-coloured grasses, including *Cortaderia selloana* 'Pumila' and *Pennisetum alopecuroides*, contrast with dark-leaved phormium and rust-coloured *Sedum* 'Herbstfreude'.

elliptica 'James Roof' and the yellow flowers of winter jasmine (*Jasminum nudiflorum*) which should be pruned after flowering as should forsythias once their early golden flowers have finished.

If you have acidic soil then the heathers are remarkable for their vivid winter colour. The three types are *Calluna*, *Daboecia* and *Erica*. Combine these plants with early-flowering camellias, rhododendrons, red-leaved pieris and skimmias with their winter berries and early flowers. There are other winter-flowering shrubs for ordinary soil including witch hazels (*Hamamelis*) that cope with all soils except poor chalky ones. Well-fed and nurtured they will bring forth early, deep yellow or orange-red flowers. *H. mollis* 'Pallida' is strongly scented and generously covered in light yellow flowers while *H.* x *intermedia* 'Diane' is deep red. All are wide-spreading and fragrant as is the neglected shrub *Lonicera purpusii* 'Winter Beauty'.

Do not forget the ornamental grasses that come into their own late in the year. The majestic cortaderias may well preen as their huge cream plumes of silky hairs survive all weathers. Beneath them varieties of *Miscanthus sinensis* with similar feathered inflorescences can be up to 1.8 m (6 ft) tall. With their parchment colouring the effect of glistening frost on them is wonderful. Other grasses such as the fountain-like *Stipa calamagrostis* have an exquisite habit and subtle colouring even in autumn. *Carex* will still be blue, silver, green or reddy-brown, *Helictotrichon sempervirens* steely blue and the slow-growing *Hakonechloa macra* 'Alboaurea' bronzed gold. When these are seen in a dusting of snow or encrusted with frost, then the excesses of summer can almost seem vulgar.

Anticipation of spring comes with the welcome appearance of the hellebores with their soft green, white and pale pink colouring. Brunneras and ferns are perfect companions as are bulbs such as snowdrops, aconites, scillas, anemones, crocus, small irises and the early species tulips that build up the colour before the full burst of spring. Winter is clearly a season for reconsidering the diversity of garden plants.

Above right

In winter the trailing flowers of *Garrya elliptica* are effectively associated with the patterns created by the frost-encrusted leaves of evergreen *Euphorbia characias wulfenii* and *Brachyglottis compacta* 'Sunshine'.

Right

Winter-flowering hellebores make a very welcome sight in every temperate garden as seen here when the lime-green flowers of *Helleborus foetidus* peer above delicate white snowdrops in late winter.

THE MOST SUITABLE
PLANTING PARTNERS

NATURAL COMPATIBILITY

So far I have been writing about plants from the artist's point of view. Making gardens is a gratifying experience and plants are a large part of the story, used in the same way as a painter's pigments or an architect's materials. We celebrate their infinite variety, help them adjust to unfamiliar surroundings and triumph over nature. But

spurred on by ecological anxiety our ideas are starting to change. There is more sensitivity towards nature and many gardeners are interested in indigenous plants that co-operate with local conditions. Nature is the ultimate creator and has much to tell us and botanically led associations – or natural compatibility – are as creative as traditional herbaceous borders, teaching us the beauty of the right plants companionably sharing the right place.

Left
Ligularias, spiraea and hemerocallis grow companionably in damp soil. Above them is golden-leaved *Robinia pseudoacacia* 'Frisia'.

Above
Opuntia, orange-flowering aloes, _Agave americana_ and _Hechtia_ thrive together in the dry heat of this San Francisco garden.

UNDERSTANDING YOUR GARDEN

The type of soil in your garden is a primary consideration when choosing naturally compatible plants. Nutrition is the key to the health of all living things. Without the right vitamins we would not survive and if you understand your own soil and plant accordingly you can expect healthy longevity from your plants.

The physical structure of your soil is as important as the chemical balance. Is your soil heavy or light or do you have the perfect loam that is somewhere between the two, easy to dig, free-draining and yet moisture-retentive? Few of us have the perfect soil so you must find out how much sand or clay your soil contains. Sand is present in all soils making them lightweight, aerated and free-draining while heavy clay-based soil is composed of fine particles. When compressed it sticks together and excludes air but retains water. Each soil has its advantages: sand has little nutritional value, dries out quickly but warms up fast in spring while mineral-rich clay can become waterlogged, remain cold and need aeration.

You can make your soil into a perfect loam by adding decayed organic matter. This helps sandy soils to retain moisture and introduces air into clay soils. Clay soils can also be improved by working in gritty materials such as coarse sand or by adding lime to make the small soil particles join together to create a crumbly medium. Alternatively, digging over clay soils before winter exposes them to frost that will break them up.

The chemical structure of your soil involves understanding what is known as the pH factor or the 'potential of hydrogen'. A pH test will indicate whether the soil is acidic or alkaline. Quite simply ericaceous or lime-hating plants will die if they are not grown in acidic soil whereas others prefer alkaline conditions. Plants for gardens with these specific soils are described later on pages 128-31. Most plants tolerate slightly acidic conditions and the ideal soil has a pH of 6.5. I do not think it is worth changing the garden's natural conditions although you can improve the soil's quality and mineral deficiencies. Working with what you have makes your garden personal so it is rarely worth attempting a fundamental soil change for one

Above

Moist, acidic conditions are suitable for *Matteuccia struthiopteris*, *Rodgersia podophylla* and *Rhododendron hunnewellianum* 'Sappho'.

Top near right

This warm south-facing house wall is ideal for grey-leaved artemisias, santolina and euphorbia as well as *Allium cristophii* and *Rosa multiflora* 'Grevillei'.

Top far right

A gravel mulch retains moisture and cools the roots of *Allium cristophii*, *Armeria maritima* 'Düsseldorf Pride' and *Salvia multicaulis*.

Right

Damp and acidic soil in light shade is perfect for *Rhododendron loderi* and the azalea *R. luteum*.

bed because the planting of the whole garden will then lack cohesion. If you wish to grow unsuitable plants then containers offer a good solution.

Daylight is also essential for plants because they feed through their leaves as well as their roots. Chlorophyll, the green pigment found in nearly all plants, enables them to use sunlight by a process known as photosynthesis in which light combines with carbon dioxide and water to produce glucose. This increases the plant's energy but means that water, taken up by the roots, is lost through the leaves as they transpire. Thus different foliage is adapted to various light conditions. In low light and damp conditions, leaves tend to be large and green. In bright light, where exposure increases the rate of transpiration, leaves are covered with fine hairs or they are economically thin. So shady areas are filled with companionably green, lushly foliaged plants while hot sunny sites have silver, slim-leaved plants.

Evolution has created plants for virtually every climate and although we have interfered with nature's selections plants have proved amazingly adaptable. Where we live may create a set of climatic constraints that restrict our choice of plants but there are areas where localized climactic areas or microclimates occur naturally and gardeners can take advantage of this. In western Ireland, for example, plants suited to hotter climates thrive despite the northern latitude because of the local warming effect of the Gulf Stream. But you can create a microclimate for specific plants such as a sunny wall for tender climbers or a raised bed for rock plants. Trees, shrubs and screens also provide shelter while our enclosed, urban gardens, insulated from weather extremes, mean that we can defy zonal authority.

PLANTING IN DIFFERENT CONDITIONS

Working with nature means accepting that plants share ecological needs including soil type, climate, aspect, exposure and light levels. If plants thrive together in the wild then they will be harmonious garden captives and this compatibility pays dividends when associating plants.

Mediterranean Gardens Mediterranean plants can live with little water, baked during long, hot summers. They enjoy being grown in gravel beds that keep their roots cool. Many of these plants also self-seed everywhere which produces beautiful results but calls for creative weeding. You can use a geo-textile sheet beneath the gravel to prevent the weeds but this removes nature's stake in the design process. The decision is up to you.

Grey-leaved olive trees symbolize the tough resilience of Mediterranean plants and look gracious among a carpet of aromatic herbage. This scented, silvery-grey vegetation is very different from that of temperate climates and includes lavenders, stachys and woolly sages. Subshrubs such as the *Perovskia atriplicifolia* have a hazier

greyness while nepeta, rosemary, thyme, rue, hyssop, curry plant and mullein add a herby note. Many are low on the ground so their textual variety is easily appreciated. You can also add some occasional splashes of brilliance from rock roses (*Helianthemum*), valerian, pastel-blue scabious, poppies and white daisies as well as perennials such as spiky echiums, agapanthus, deep blue anchusa and *Euphorbia characias wulfenii*.

For the larger garden, sculptural shapes such as large spiky leaves, fanning palms, spiny cacti and the Italian cypress (*Cupressus sempervirens* 'Stricta') also create a Mediterranean scenario. Spiky yuccas can also be combined with a variety of palms to create bold images. Include 'exotics' like flowering candelabra aloes to add a sub-tropical note. The fleshy, water-conserving succulents are successful as are the aggressive agaves with

Above left
These perennial cacti known as *Cleisocactus* 'Rojo Card' look dramatic beside the rock face.
Below
***Papaver orientale* 'Juliane', *Anthemis punctata cupaniana* and *Agave americana* enjoy the dry conditions in this garden.**

Left
This dry garden contains *Yucca gloriosa*, *Senecio mandraliscae* and *Aloe saponaria*.
Below
A classic combination of agaves and kniphofias.

their sculptural demonstrative forms. Cacti are static plants with shapes ranging from squat, rounded prickly domes to ribbed columns.

Trees and shrubs for dry sites include golden mimosa, fluffy albizia, violet-blue jacaranda and pink tamarisk, all of which flower prolifically. A flowering middle layer might also include hibicus, daphne, oleander, buddleja, cistus, ceanothus, potentillas and myrtle (*Myrtus*). Climbing bougainvillea, plumbago, solanum and wistaria could be added. These plants often have aromatic foliage or fragrant flowers, a joy in a Mediterranean garden. The garden style can be achieved by mixing the plants just described but it depends on your soil and level of exposure. Instead, opt for plants with cool green, glaucous or jade-green foliage.

117

A Temperate Gravel Garden This circular bed is part of an intimate town garden that receives plenty of sunshine and the plants have been selected accordingly. The moisture-retaining gravel surface is an excellent alternative to a lawn, for which this garden is perhaps too small, and provides free drainage for plants that originate from rather arid regions, whether they are native species or hybrids raised by nurserymen. Gravel has the added advantage of acting as a weed suppressor.

The look created in this garden is very natural although the self-seeding plants call for a degree of control. To keep the circular gravel area as free of transgressing plants as possible there is a plastic membrane beneath much of the central area through which no plant is able to take root. The central space thus remains clear but is encircled by a plantable ring, without a membrane, of soil topped with gravel.

The design is very simple in approach with clipped domes of box (*Buxus sempervirens*) performing a stabilizing, architectural role, arranged at regular intervals around the circular perimeter and as a solid mass beneath the bench. In nearbys beds there are more structured plants including sedums, euphorbias, acanthus, spartium and aralia. Ground-covering epimediums and geraniums work in beneath the taller plants and massed purple sage (*Salvia officinalis* Purpurascens Group) is often repeated.

Year One

Although symmetry is a large part of the design nature dominates the overall look of the garden. Plants noted for their efficient seed dispersal, such as *Alchemilla mollis*, *Eschscholzia californica*, *Viola labradorica* and *Stipa gigantea*, are actively encouraged. The plants are perfectly suited to the sun-filled site with free-draining soil and so the scheme is self-sustaining to some extent. The artist-designer simply completes nature's picture.

KEY *(H = Height; S = Spread)*

1. *Santolina pinnata neapolitana* 'Edward Bowles', *H: 75 cm (2½ ft); S: 90 cm (3 ft)*

2. *Miscanthus sacchariflorus*, *H: 2.5 m (8 ft); S: 90 cm (3 ft)*

3. *Cytisus battandieri*, *H: 5 m (16 ft); S: 3.7 m (12 ft)*

4. *Sedum* 'Herbstfreude', *H and S: 60 cm (2 ft)*

5. *Melianthus major*, *H and S: 2-3 m (6-10 ft)*

6. *Macleaya cordata*, *H: 1.5 m (5 ft); S: 60 cm (2 ft)*

7. *Phlomis fruticosa*, *H: 90 cm (3 ft); S: 75 cm (2½ ft)*

8. *Coreopsis verticillata* 'Moonbeam', *H: 40-60 cm (16-24 in); S: 30 cm (1 ft)*

9. *Salvia officinalis* Purpurascens Group, *H: 60 cm (2 ft); S: 90 cm (3 ft)*

10. *Allium cristophii*, *H: 15-40 cm (6-16 in); S: 15-20 cm (6-8 in)*

11. *Spartium junceum*, *H and S: 3 m (10 ft)*

12. *Rudbeckia fulgida deamii*, *H: 90 cm (3 ft); S: 60 cm (2 ft)*

13. *Euphorbia griffithii* 'Fireglow', *H: 90 cm (3 ft); S: 50 cm (20 in)*

14. *Phyllostachys nigra*, *H: 6-8 m (20-25 ft); S: indefinite*

15. *Acanthus spinosus*, *H: 1.2 m (4 ft); S: 60 cm (2 ft)*

16. *Buddleja davidii* 'Black Knight', *H and S: 5 m (16 ft)*

17. *Aralia elata*, *H and S: 10 m (30 ft)*

18. *Epimedium* x *perralchicum*,

H: 45 cm (1½ ft); S: 30 cm (1 ft)

19. *Foeniculum vulgare* 'Purpureum', *H: 1.8 m (6 ft); S: 45 cm (1½ ft)*

20. *Rosa* 'Louis XIV', *H: 1.2 m (4 ft); S: 45 cm (1½ ft)*

21. *Hemerocallis* 'Stafford', *H: 75 cm (2½ ft); S: 60 cm (2 ft)*

22. *Buxus sempervirens*, *H and S: 45 cm (1½ ft)*

23. *Alchemilla mollis*, *H and S: 50 cm (20 in)*

24. *Stipa gigantea*, *H: 2.5 m (8 ft); S: 90 cm (3 ft)*

25. *Viola labradorica*, *H: 2.5-5 cm (1-2 in); S: indefinite*

26. *Potentilla* 'Gibson's Scarlet', *H and S: 45 cm (1½ ft)*

27. *Eschscholzia californica*, *H: 30 cm (1 ft); S: 15 cm (6 in)*

28. Runner beans, *H: 2.5 m (8 ft)*

29. *Euphorbia amygdaloides robbiae*, *H: 45-60 cm (1½-2 ft); S: 60 cm (2 ft)*

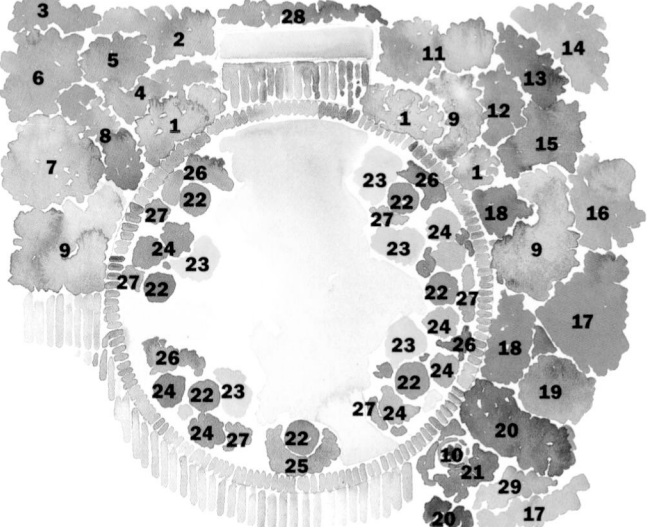

Year one, left The garden is shown here in the summer, and the permanent plants in the surrounding beds are beginning to become established while those plants within the circular gravel area, including lady's mantle (*Alchemilla mollis*), California poppy (*Eschscholzia californica*), the ornamental grass *Stipa gigantea* and *Viola labradorica* are starting to sow their seed. Although this is the garden's first summer the attractive colour scheme is already beginning to show. This is due to the strongly coloured plants such as *Potentilla* 'Gibson's Scarlet', mahogany daylilies (*Hemerocallis* 'Stafford'), the burnt-orange *Euphorbia griffithi* 'Fireglow', golden-yellow *Phlomis fruticosa*, primrose-yellow *Coreopsis verticillata* 'Moonbeam' and bronze fennel (*Foeniculum vulgare* 'Purpureum').

Year Two

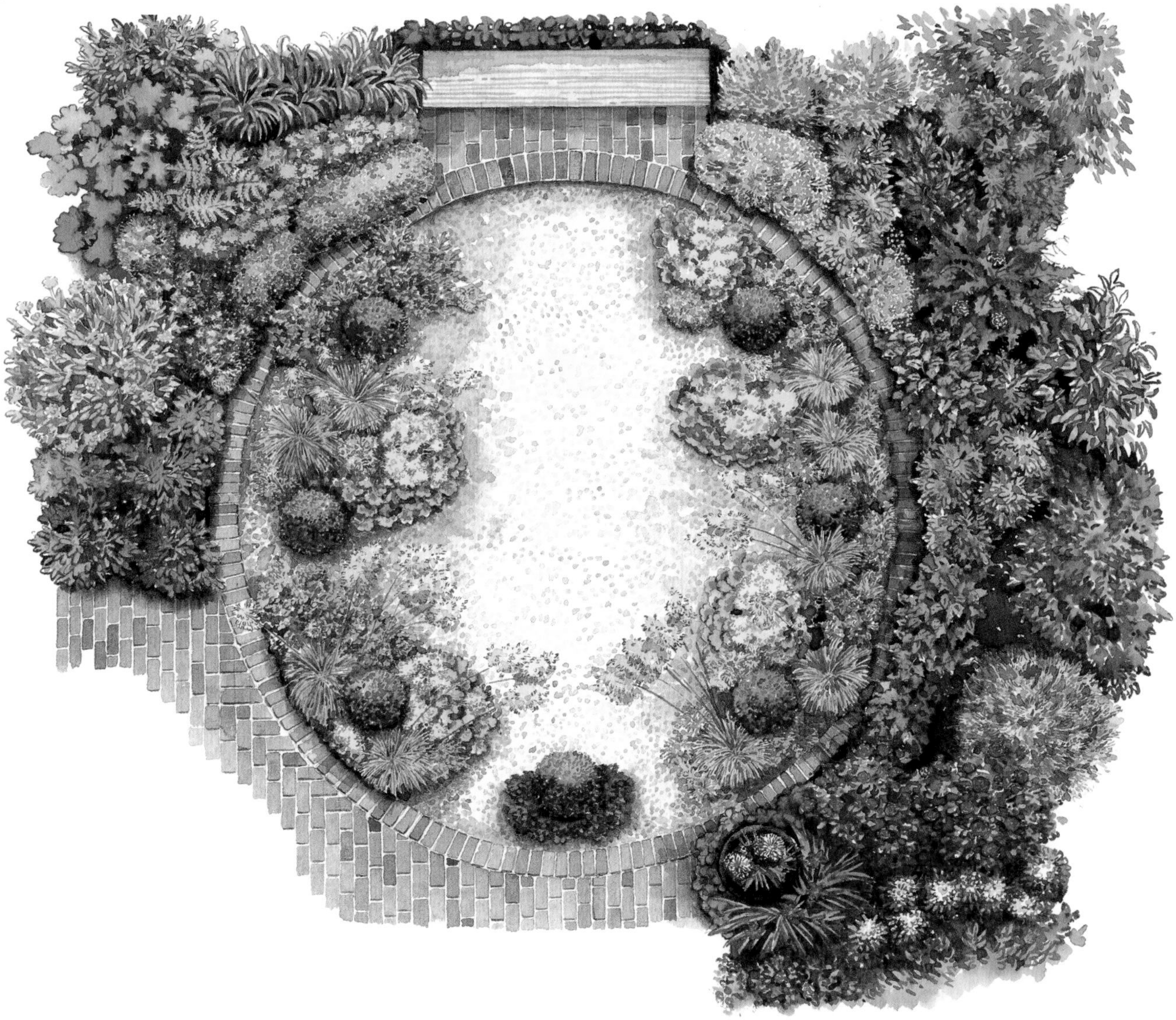

Year three, above This view of the garden shows how suited it is for a small area, even in a town garden. The whole design has been planted close to the house walls and garden fencing in order to create a sense of quiet, intimate seclusion. To enhance the feeling of natural abandon the boundary fence has also been planted with a selection of climbers such as *Cobaea scandens*, with its bell-shaped green then white flowers, *Solanum crispum* 'Glasnevin' and *Clematis* 'Jackmanii'.

Year two, left The garden is shown here in its second summer. By this time the shimmering flower heads of the ornamental grass *Stipa gigantea* are still more apparent and are starting to dominate the scene along with masses of foaming yellow *Alchemilla mollis* at foot. The gold and orange California poppy has seeded generously around the perimeter of the gravelled area while the red potentillas and the delicate orange flowers of *Hemerocallis* 'Stafford' add colourful details that tone well with the inflorescences of the elegant ornamental grasses.

Woodland Gardens It is surprisingly easy to achieve a natural effect when gardening in woodland because the plants are biased towards foliage rather than flowers. Although trees provide winter protection it is important to establish the degree of shade as well as the soil type. In deciduous woods the maximum light occurs in early spring when bulbs such as *Anemone blanda*, *Galanthus elwesii*, English bluebells (*Hyacinthoides non-scripta*) and *Cyclamen coum* provide the colour. Densely planted trees should include wondrous glades in the design while dappled light and the brighter light at the woodland edge mean more garden varieties can be grown. By early summer, the tree canopy is established for the season and the pattern of dense shade or filtered light will stay the same until autumn.

Really dense shade is the most difficult to plant beneath but grasses like sedge (*Carex plantaginea*), wavy hair grass (*Deschampsia flexuosa*) or greater woodrush (*Luzula sylvatica*) can be grown with ground ivy and frondy ferns. In less heavy shade, the aim should be to suggest natural plant communities without concentrating on wild species alone. In your woodland area, you may have lungwort, woodruff, solomon's seal and lords and ladies,

Above
Anemones (*Anemone blanda*) carpet the ground with pretty daisy flowers creating a splash of blue and white. They are ideal ground-covering plants for this site as they prefer the light shade found at the woodland edge.

Inset, right
In the early spring, these white drifts of delicate *Galanthus nivalis* have naturalised among carpets of the lovely, sunshine-yellow flowers of winter aconites (*Eranthis hyemalis*).

for example. To these can be added grasses, monkshoods, ferns, spurges, foxgloves and primulas as well as hellebores for early-flowering interest. In a more planned woodland garden, shrubs such as *Prunus laurocerasus* forms, dogwoods, elders, viburnums and evergreen aucubas add bulk and if the soil is acidic you may like to include rhododendrons and azaleas.

The low-level planting can be particularly seductive. Good companions for semi-natural woodland include spring violets, the Gladwin iris (*Iris foetidissima*) with its orange winter fruits, blue-flowered *Brunnera macrophylla* and drifts of white lily-of-the-valley (*Convallaria majalis*). At the woodland edge, garden cultivars such as *Geranium sylvaticum*, *G. macrorrhizum* and Martagon lily (*Lilium martagon*) would not be out of place. At the end of summer, *Anemone* x *hybrida* and the gently coloured garden forms of astilbes, hostas and campanulas would blend in well. When selecting garden cultivars remember that woodland colours should be low-key rather than brightly coloured so that they merge well with the textured foliage of your woodland.

Main picture, left

There is perhaps no more uplifting experience in the spring than the sight of a woodland covered with a fragrant blue carpet of nodding English bluebells (*Hyacinthoides non-scripta*).

Below

Late spring marks the appearance of the white- and purple-chequered flowers of snakeshead fritillaries (*Fritillaria meleagris*). Here they are associated with *Leucojum aestivum*, *Narcissus bulbocodium* and cardamines.

Wildflower Gardens Images of the wild are but interpretations, made with the intention of fostering an illusion. Wildflower meadows are popular but they require an understanding of soil type and the local microclimate as well as the specific needs of wild flowers. Not all will be possible in your own site. Natural wildflower communities suited to the locale are ideal. Although they need thorough maintenance the rewards are exquisite.

To create a wildflower meadow remove the topsoil to leave a poor subsoil which imitates a meadow's thin, nutrient-starved soil. The soil will be bursting with potential life so let the land lie fallow for a year, systemically kill any unwanted plants and choose a wildflower and grass mix from a specialist. The mix will mainly depend on whether your soil is chalky, damp, dry, sandy or acidic. For example, agrimony, ox-eye daisy, knapweed, white clover, meadow sweet, scabious, tansy, valerian and vetch prefer limy soil while mildly acidic soils support betony, cornflower, daisies, forget-me-nots, harebells, wild pansies and poppies. In damp, clay soils plant campion, cowslip, meadow cranesbill, selfheal and yarrow.

Sow the seed in prepared, raked soil in the autumn and cut down three times in the first year. The meadow will develop a natural balance with the strong overtaking the weak which is where you might intervene, adding 'plugs' of compatible plants. Bearing in mind that all garden plants originate from wild species extend the season by adding subtle cultivars of compatible plants such as elders, hawthorn, Guelder rose, willows, dogwoods and honeysuckle.

The tamed wild plants of an American prairie garden are very different. Prairie landscapes are adapted to exposed conditions and, as a result, native plants are deeply rooted and independent. Choose a few species rather than over- complicating the plan with dot effects. Three types of grass to nine broad-leaved perennials will create a prairie image. Buy seed that can cope with the conditions from local suppliers and think in terms of informal, flowing drifts that grade in colour with grass textures as a continuum. At first maintenance involves a balancing act so that the fast-growing grasses do not drown out the perennials until they are stronger.

The species grasses, red switch grass (*Panicum virgatum*), bluestem (*Andropogon gerardii*), and non-native wild grasses like fountain grass (*Pennisetum alopecuroides*) are ideal. Perennial partners include Texas bluebonnet, *Rudbeckia fulgida deamii*, pink loosestrife with Joe Pye weed (*Eupatorium purpureum*) for pattern, texture and colour. Always remember to check local conditions and work generously: hesitation and small thinking are not appropriate.

Above
California poppies (*Eschscholzia californica*) are successfully associated with *Sidalcea malviflora*.
Left
Prairie verbenas have been planted among delicate, yellow square bud primroses.
Right
Texas bluebonnets blend beautifully with pink evening primrose (*Oenothera speciosa*).
Main picture, right
A wild bank of buttercups and dandelion seedheads typifies an English meadow.
Inset, far right
These *Iris douglasiana* and bright orange *Eschscholzia californica* look lovely in a meadow.

Bog Gardens Permanently wet areas invite lush foliage plants and visually subordinate flowers apart from primulas, lythrums, trollius, astilbes, marsh marigolds (*Caltha palustris*) and iris. Unless you have a naturally wet area, you must create an artificial bog – there are many different methods so ask an expert. You should also assess how much shade will protect your bog because it slows down the rate of transpiration, which is particularly important for larger plants.

The size of your wet area, whether it be alongside a natural stream or around a pool, will also affect the type of plants. *Gunnera manicata* suits large sites but not the average domestic plot and I have reservations about extraordinary plants in a simple non-native habitat. Yet there are other unconventional plants, such as *Rheum palmatum* 'Atrosanguineum', with deeply cut leaves, which blend in easily while still adding accent to the scene. Plants that prefer wetter conditions include round-leaved umbrella plant (*Darmera peltata*, syn. *Peltiphyllum peltatum*) with its pale pink flowers. Acidic bog is ideal for the splendid royal fern (*Osmunda regalis*) and the ostrich fern (*Matteuccia struthiopteris*). To complement these powerful shapes add the lance-leaved flag iris (*Iris pseudacorus*), cream-flowered goat's beard (*Aruncus dioicus*) and pink-flowered Joe Pye weed (*Eupatorium purpureum*). Some huge-leaved hostas such as blueish *Hosta sieboldiana* and the glossily green *H.* 'Royal Standard' with its white flowers also merge neatly in such company.

If you have space, a wild look can be achieved using shrub willows and dogwoods with the fern-like leaves of meadowsweets such as *Filipendula rubra* 'Venusta' from the American prairies. If carefully managed, you can include drifts of invasive plants such as the lovely cream-striped grass *Glyceria maxima* variegata, the lesser reedmace (*Typha angustifolia*) and *Persicaria bistorta* 'Superba' as well as marsh marigolds (*Caltha palustris*), flowering rush (*Butomus umbellatus*), *Calla palustris* and blue-flowered water forget-me-nots (*Myosotis scorpioides*).

Be very wary of using wild-looking, rampant plants if you have a small garden. Instead you should consider massing larger and smaller hostas, astilbes, trollius, daylilies and drifts of primulas. *Primula japonica*, the giant Himalayan cowslip (*P. florindae*) and the smaller, sweetly scented yellow *P. sikkimensis* are particularly attractive. You might also try the fluffy, white panicles of acid-loving *Smilacena racemosa* and

Main picture, right
A damp site is ideal for these dark and pale pink candelabra primulas in association with yellow-flowered globeflowers (*Trollius*), ligularias and the dramatic leaves of the moisture-loving hostas.

Below
The many plants thriving in this lush bog garden include *Rheum palmatum*, hostas, white-flowered astilbes and tall, yellow *Iris pseudacorus*.

Above

The mildy acidic, damp conditions of this garden, whose plants tumble over the water's edge, mean brightly coloured *Rhododendron luteum* has pale pink polygonums, hostas and an acer for company.

Inset, left

This cream-and-green grass, *Glyceria maxima*, prefers these damp conditions and looks well associated with yellow globeflowers (*Trollius*).

dramatic rodgersia leaves with frothy cream or pink flower spikes. The round-leaved ligularias such as *Ligularia dentata* 'Desdemona' can also be incorporated. Ligularias often have dark, pewter-maroon leaves and tousled, orange daisy-like flowers clustering above their foliage. *L.* 'The Rocket' is different, however, with lemon-yellow spires and black stems that reach nearly 1.8 m (6 ft) tall above heart-shaped, serrated leaves. Merge in tall ferns, clumps of *Iris sibirica*, some magnificent cimicifugas as well as the beautiful red cardinal flower (*Lobelia cardinalis*) which originates from North East America.

Coastal Gardens Wind, the gardener's enemy, is the most influential factor when selecting plants for gardens beside the ocean. Windbreaks are a prerequisite although they can conceal a beautiful vista. Bear in mind too that coastal winds are salt-laden while the soil is often sandy

Above

Dramatically fan-shaped leaves of Chusan or windmill palms (*Trachycarpus fortunei*) combined with cordylines and yuccas work very well together as they line the sandy pathway. They all enjoy the warm conditions of this garden situated on the south-west coast of England.

Near right

Red-edged, grass-like leaves of *Dyckia fosteriana* are flattered by their association with succulent *Sedum acre* and *S. palmeri* in this free-draining soil with a gravel mulch.

Far right

In a coastal garden, this paved pathway leads down enticingly to the Mediterranean and is edged with masses of purple-flowered *Echium fastuosum* and silver *Ballota acetabulosa* as well as the highly fragrant *Lavandula stoechas*.

and lacking in nutrients. Seashore plants tend to be low-growing and if you try to dig one up you will encounter a deep root system that enables the first rank of salt-tolerant plants to stand firm. Behind them *Leymus arenarius* and the marram grass (*Ammophila arenaria*) hold coastal dunes against the drag of waves.

The green-and-yellow cord grass (*Spartina pectinata* 'Aureomarginata') and the green-and-white gardener's garters (*Phalaris arundinacea picta*) also cope with seashore conditions and make good accent grasses. These plants could be used to repeat a grass-like pattern elsewhere in the garden. You should also consider using ornamental grasses and sedges among the perennials. Fescues will mass well to create small mounds while feather grasses could add taller, flowering textures.

As you move away from the water's edge the soil improves although it will still be sandy and fast-draining. Even after rain the wind dries the soil surface instantly so most of the plants must be drought-tolerant. You may need to improve your soil over the years, using grasses to hold it and digging in bulky organic material. In the open garden you should concentrate on plants related to native flora, aiming for a lot of cover to prevent erosion and in successive years replace lost planting with your choice of perennials.

Despite these constraints, seashore plants create an unusual and coherent style of garden. Gardening beside the coast also ensures a moderate climate and less chance of extreme cold although this depends on where you live. Mild climates, such as hot Mediterranean coastal gardens, expand planting opportunities while you will find humid air and bright light an asset.

So inland from the grasses, where there is more chance of a good loam, you can compile a comprehensive perennial list including the prickly sea hollies (*Eryngium*), thrifts (*Armeria maritima*) and blue *Iris douglasiana* that relate to indigenous plants. *Echium* and *Limonium platyphyllum* with massed pale blue and lilac flowers above dark leathery leaves also suit the theme. Lupins, crocosmia, anaphalis, blue or cream scabious, globe thistles (*Echinops*), *Echinacea*, lantanas as well as osteospermums and gazanias make attractive additions.

So there are two ways of planting in maritime areas. You can opt for the perennials described, planting in loose flowing groups or create a semi-concealed microclimate where tender plants are sheltered by protective, wind-resistant, preferably evergreen shrubs such as flowering escallonias, griselinias, pittosporums, rosemary, hydrangea, fuchsia, potentilla, lavender and lavatera, all of which are also highly decorative.

Gardens with Acidic Soil These lime-free soils have a pH of 6.9 down to 4.5, a reading that suggests acidic, poorly drained peat although acidic soils can also be sandy or clay-based. Test the soil if you are unsure and look at the plants already growing there. For example, bracken, nettles, trilliums and heaths found on moorland or woodland all indicate acidity. In gardens, acid-loving evergreens such as rhododendrons, pieris, skimmias, magnolias and camellias are an asset. Heathers are ground covers for exposed heaths and cannot be omitted in a section on acid soils. They are ideal for some town gardens where carefully judged selections provide colour all year.

Some trees revel in acidity but vary in their other needs. *Stewartia pseudocamellia* with its white flowers, the bells of *Styrax japonicus*, the vermilion flowers of the evergreen Chilean fire bush (*Embothrium coccineum*) and ivory-flowered *Drimys winteri* in late spring prefer damp

light woodland. Birches, chestnuts and robinias prefer drier conditions while many great conifers like acid soils although the physical structure of the soil must also be considered. But it is the rhododendrons and their close associates the azaleas that are seen as leaders among acid-loving plants. In acidic, moist, free-draining soil

Above
Acidic soil is vital for *Erica carnea* 'Pink Spangles', *E. c.* 'Springwood White' and *E. c.* 'Vivellii'.
Main picture, right
This pathway of azaleas and rhododendrons would not be possible without acidic soil.
Far right
This bluebell field is enhanced by the view of Ghent azaleas in the distance.

with plenty of humus they produce sumptuous flower trusses in many colours. They range in size from tree-like to dwarf and, like perennials, the larger their leaves the more shade they require. The 15 m (50 ft) tall *Rhododendron sinogrande* is a great woodland tree while *R. macabeanum* has yellow flowers. *R. cinnabarinum,* with blueish foliage and tubular pendant flowers, is a more

Above
Clump-forming *Trillium sessile* with reddish-brown flowers is accompanied by yellow *Erythronium* 'Pagoda' and *Anemone nemorosa*.

manageable size as are the *R. yakushimanum* hybrids and dwarf *R. impeditum* in colours such as red, pink, yellow, creamy blue and white.

Azaleas tend to be hotter hued, often with outstanding autumn colour. Choose from sun-loving deciduous azaleas like pink *Rhododendron austrinum* 'Betty Anne Voss' or shade-loving evergreen azaleas in cooler, blue-toned reds or pinks such as *R. hunnewellianum* 'Blue Danube' or warmer shades like *R. h.* Gibraltar Group. Acidic-loving shrubs to partner them might include the white *Exochorda* x *macrantha* 'The Bride', blue-white, pink and red camellias, the calico bush (*Kalmia latifolia*) and the beauty bush (*Kolkwitzia amabilis*). *Fothergilla major* with its fragrant white flowers and deep pink *Clethra alnifolia* 'Rosea' are also good planting companions. In lightly wooded areas that have damp, acidic soil these shrubs look very attractive with ferns, bluebells, arums, foxgloves and some lilies.

Gardens with Alkaline Soil Alkaline soils have a pH of 7.1 upwards and usually occur where the geological profile is chalky or made of limestone bedrock. The soil is thin, dry and low in iron and magnesium and plants unable to obtain these from alkaline soils become chlorotic. The cruciferae, clematis, helianthemums, scabious, iris and most of the pink family (*Dianthus*) are naturally suited to draining, alkaline soils. It is better to work with your soil although improvements are worth the effort. You can dig in manure or leaf-

Main picture, left
Herbaceous plants thrive in this well-worked, chalky garden and include tall, white foxgloves (*Digitalis*), dark blue *Campanula persicifolia* and delicate, pink dianthus.

Inset, left
Phlox, erigerons and acanthus grow successfully together in these mildly alkaline conditions.

Below
This border contains chalk-based soil which is ideal for these mainly pink-flowered plants such as penstemons, achilleas, salvias and grey-leaved Scotch thistle (*Onopordum acanthium*).

mould to improve the soil's structure, alkalinity and capacity to hold water and nutrients. Incorporate composted organic material every year and add sequestered iron and a little balanced fertilizer a few times during the growing season.

There is a lengthy list of plants for these conditions apart from the true calcifuges. Select even-tempered, lime-tolerant shrubs such as berberis, pyracanthas and buddlejas. Massed foliage such as smoke tree (*Cotinus coggygria*) also provides a good backdrop. Sun-loving *Ceanothus* and the *Cistus* family flower gloriously in slightly alkaline, free-draining soil. In late summer you can also depend on the flowering beauty of *Hibiscus syriacus* with white, pink or blue flowers.

Scented shrubs such as lilacs (*Syringa*) tolerate alkalinity. Purple *S. vulgaris* 'Charles Joly' or the compact *S. microphylla* 'Superba' can be combined with fragrant *Philadelphus* 'Beauclerk' or *P.* 'Virginal'. The sweet bay (*Laurus nobilis*) has glossy, aromatic leaves while the white flowers of sweet box (*Sarcococca hookeriana humilis*) fill the winter garden with their scent.

Having established a shrub framework there are many perennials that can be used to lighten the summer months including yarrows such as *Achillea filipendulina* 'Gold Plate' and the paler *A.* 'Moonshine' whose flat flower heads contrast with upright, blue *Salvia nemorosa* 'East Friesland' and the spires of *Veronica spicata* cultivars.

Carnations and pinks need ample lime to produce their great variety of foliage and flower as do blue *Scabiosa caucasica* 'Clive Greaves' and white *S. c.* 'Miss Willmott' which can also be creamy yellow or pink. Blue campanulas enjoy alkaline soils: *Campanula persicifolia* is delicately structured, *C. lactiflora* 'Prichard's Variety' is

luscious while *C. l.* 'Loddon Anna' has pinkish overtones. The pink and white flowers of valerian (*Centranthus ruber*) and those of hazy gypsophila will also work in well. Unlike many other species of iris that prefer moist conditions, *Iris germanica* hybrids appreciate lime and good drainage. If you enrich the soil you can also grow chrysanthemums, geraniums, sidalceas, phlox, rudbeckias, verbascums, perovskias, poppies, kniphofias, cheiranthus and solidago. By the autumn the

Above
The dry, alkaline soil in this garden bed provides the ideal growing conditions for stachys, echiums, helichrysum and the dried seed-heads of alliums.

Michaelmas daisies (*Aster*) are in full flower. They grow well in limy soil although they need more moisture, and are really summer's last fling.

It is also worth adding bulbs to this herbaceous mix. They need good drainage and so can cope with alkaline soils as long as they are not clay-based. The Asiatic lilies such as white *Lilium nepalense* are ideal and in light, draining soil alliums add form and texture.

GROWTH, SIZE AND HABIT

When designing with plants the passing of time must be written into the programme from the outset. Plants are frequently planted too close together although this mistake may not be evident for ten years or, in the case of trees, a lifetime. So designing with growing material means that time should be one of our main considerations.

In grand schemes we owe it to the future to plan beyond our own lifetime while in more local time we may want a three-year effect or longer. Mull over the life expectancy of each of your plants, particularly the trees and shrubs, and allow nature to co-direct your design. Plants have a will of their own, ranging from the wandering honeysuckle to journeying ground-covers, and the ability to manipulate this natural beauty is the gardener's gift.

Left
The concept behind this Japanese-style garden is to curb the natural growth habit of plants such as pines and juniper with careful pruning.

Above
Permanent plants such as *Rosa* 'Elizabeth of Glamis', *Lavandula stoechas* and eryngiums are assisted by self-sown *Alchemilla mollis* and alliums.

AN INTRODUCTION TO GROWTH RATES

All living things have a predetermined genetic growth pattern with plants programmed for different conditions. Restful gardens contain contented plants that have sufficient space to develop their own characteristic habit to the full without being gradually consumed by the surrounding plants.

Many shrubs may in fact be regarded as trees. Indeed, magnolias can reach up to 6 m (20 ft) tall while the red buckeye (*Aesculus pavia* 'Atrosanguinea') will grow to 5 m (15 ft) although it is clothed to the ground like a shrub. Other shrubs spread as widely sideways as they aspire upwards. Medium-sized shrubs such as spring-yellow *Corylopsis pauciflora*, the evergreen *Prunus laurocerasus* 'Otto Luyken' and witch hazels (*Hamamelis*) all expand sideways. Many hydrangeas, shrub willows and viburnums also have a wide-spreading, branching habit. In contrast, the herbaceous perennials display a range of different habits. There are narrow verticals such as foxgloves and irises as well as perennials such as hostas, bergenias and brunneras that cover the ground, suppressing competition with their layering foliage. Some herbaceous plants such as peonies grow in clumps that gradually expand while others like strawberries (*Fragaria*) spread by runners, which are horizontal stems that root as they touch down.

Below the ground, roots anchor the plant and search for food, either growing down deeply or horizontally. Above ground level, light draws the plants ever upwards so that even horizontal growers can maximize the amount of light they receive and so display their wares. The extent of a plant's growth is linked with levels of light, water, minerals and oxygen and we can supply all these needs to ensure healthy, optimum growth. In fact, a tradition has emerged whereby we improve the soil, pour in fertilizer and encourage luxurious growth. Some plants grow faster and more strongly than others but survival of the fittest is not a good philosophy in the garden unless you want nettles and docks. As garden directors we can restrict overbearing or exceptionally successful plants by checking their progress.

Above left
Glorious displays of colour in the summer from this planting of rudbeckias, achilleas, montbretias and heleniums will soon give way to the die-back and parchment-like colours that are typical of late autumnal herbaceous plants.

Left
The permanence of trees and shrubs can be invaluable throughout the year although this deciduous, spreading *Catalpa bignonioides* 'Aurea' is slow to develop leaves and loses them relatively early in the autumn.

Unchecked, plants such as *Geranium macrorrhizum* or grasses like *Phalaris arundinacea picta* make good ground cover but being rhizomatous they swallow up all in their path. But there are also some very vigorous perennials that can be contained if they are grown in a competitive situation to produce a self-regulating planting pattern. So rampant spreading plants such as *Alchemilla mollis* establish a truce with *Euphorbia amygdaloides robbiae*.

Plants do not read. They do not know that they are meant to reach a pre-scribed size and shape. Some do not even know when they are supposed to die, living far longer than we expected. We 'know' because experts have writ-ten about these characteristics. You will notice that on occasion I have given plant sizes. I am trying to be helpful but I am quite sure that all readers will have different experiences of the same plant that will contradict what they read. We are not dealing with absolutes – as I have said, nature should co-direct as we develop our gardens.

When well situated and well suited to the conditions in which they are grown, plants can thrive and reach magnificent proportions. A good example is *Phormium tenax*. This plant reaches a magnificent 3 m (10 ft) in its native New Zealand whereas in less ideal British conditions it grows to only 1.8 m (6 ft). Conversely, we have all seen plants with stunted growth, usually due to strong winds or nutrient starvation although deliberately stunting a plant's growth or *bonsai* is also an art form in Japan. We can inhibit growth by pro-viding poor conditions and even 'improve' flowering by the same manner. Children notice how the seeds of annual nasturtiums produce far more flow-ers when planted in thin, poor soil compared with rich humus in which they will not bother to flower. So if you are gardening in sympathy with your plants and providing continuously for all their needs the rewards should exceed your expectations. Your plants may achieve heights or spreads far larger than anticipated. You can but try to site plants where they are happiest and work with them companionably and logically.

Above right

Striking yellow-and-green foliage of *Astrantia major* 'Sunningdale Variegated' extends its decorative impact while golden-coloured *Ribes* and yellow *Spiraea* foliage add further valuable colour to the scene.

Right

Conifers provide year-round impact because of their different shades of green, blue and silver. They offer great variety of interesting forms, including weeping, dome-shaped and horizontal, as well as having invitingly tactile and richly varied visual textures.

PRIMARY AND SECONDARY PLANTING

Creating an enduring image to stir the senses involves making pragmatic decisions. Respecting the ever-changing character of growing plants and allowing them ample space will result in successful planting companionships. Some plants reach adolescence remarkably fast while others hesitate for years before putting on a growth spurt. Tackling these constraints, however, provides an opportunity for temporary planting.

Think of planting in layers in terms of both height and spread. Primary plants such as trees add a look of instant maturity, particularly if you buy larger stock. Even small gardens acquire a feeling of permanence if a small, ornamental flowering tree is included while larger gardens can accommodate oaks, ash or beech. As a sense of proportion is also important you must consider the tree's ultimate height and spread.

The siting of trees also creates light or shady areas in the garden and so influences your other plant choices. Birches, eucalyptus, the golden-rain tree (*Koelreuteria paniculata*), *Amelanchier lamarckii* and the tree of heaven (*Ailanthus altissima*), for example, become established very quickly. Slow-starting trees such as the Japanese maples (*Acer*), *Ginkgo* and the dove tree (*Davidia involucrata*) may need time as well as enough space to make their impact. If you do not wish to wait for trees to reach their ultimate size, plant fast-growing shrubs in the vicinity as a temporary measure to create mass and shade. But make sure that they do not compete with the growing tree for light, air and water.

Shrubs make up the second group of primary plants. Again you must consider their expected mass at ten years old so that you can space

them well when planting. Large shrubs include the wonderfully fragrant lilacs and philadelphus as well as buddlejas, lavateras, cotoneasters and pyracanthas. The large *Viburnum rhytidophyllum*, *Chimonanthus praecox*, the northern bayberry *Myrica pensylvanica* and the contorted white mulberry (*Morus alba*) all have a distinctive character. They form the backbone of the garden but their rate of growth and lifespan will vary. Buddlejas, kerria, pyracantha, the Cornelian cherry

Above

Trees and shrubs provide a backing for euphorbia and *Alchemilla mollis* and many other herbaceous plants during the summer progression.

Top near right

This hedge is a backdrop for *Rosa* 'Pink Bells' and *R.* 'Tuscany Superb'. *Alchemilla mollis* and eryngiums add quickly effective summer colour.

Top far right

Pale purple delphiniums add height very quickly to a summer border and are echoed further down by the upright flowers of kniphofia.

Right

From a wooden seat the view of this verdant garden will change rapidly throughout the season. By the end of the summer, *Macleaya cordata* has grown very tall and *Hydrangea paniculata* also attracts a great deal of attention.

(*Cornus mas*) and many shrub roses are fast-growers while magnolias, pieris, Oregon grape (*Mahonia aquifolium*) and Japanese acers are slow-starters. Gardeners cannot indulge their impatience because they would lose some beautiful opportunities. It is better to include slower plants and to use annuals, perennials and bulbs as fillers, reducing their number as the shrubs fill their allotted space in the first four or five years.

Smaller shrubs such as lavenders, deutzias, daphnes, potentillas, cistus and long-flowering 'patio' or 'landscape' roses are secondary in the order of things. They are the decorative icing on the cake unlike the formative space dividers, the primary plants. Secondary plants create patterns, textures and colours, quickly covering the soil with foliage and flowers within the first three years. They are mainly herbaceous perennials although annuals, biennials, tender perennials and bulbs all have a role to play. Some are naturally vigorous which means that we must intervene if they exclude slower colleagues. So after two to three years you may split any large masses in autumn. Many low ground-covers such as tiarellas, geraniums, lily-of-the-valley (*Convallaria majalis*), sweet woodruff (*Galium odoratum*), lilyturf (*Liriope*) and *Ajania pacifica* quickly conceal the soil. Rhizomatous grasses do the same but do not know when to stop.

In shady conditions, given good soil that does not dry out, Japanese anemones, astrantias, daylilies (*Hemerocallis*), acanthus, ligularias and astilbes will all grow very quickly. In hotter, drier conditions, artemisias cover the ground surprisingly fast as do the spurges (*Euphorbia*). These include architectural *Euphorbia characias* and spreading *E. griffithi* 'Fireglow'. Revelling in the

heat, *Sedum* 'Herbstfreude' also quickly forms large clumps while rudbeckias spread by rhizomes in moisture-retentive soil. In similar conditions, Joe Pye weed (*Eupatorium purpureum*) will also rapidly fill spaces. For sword-like foliage the vigorous *Iris pseudacorus* and crocosmias produce quick results. Herbaceous phlox are also a delight in every garden, providing substantial mounds that often reach 90 cm (3 ft) tall. These include pure white *Phlox paniculata* 'Fujiyama' and lavender *P. p.* 'Caroline van den Berg'.

Plants that spread by seed can also grow substantially, even in two years. Valerian, sisyrinchiums, alchemillas, aquilegias and lavateras are good examples. In the border, weeding is an ever present chore for the first couple of years but it is worth keeping the soil clean for the benefit of the perennials. They will start suppressing weeds themselves and then 'hands-on' selective weeding will remove plants as they invade neighbouring space.

Left
A lush summer effect is produced using *Atriplex bortensis rubra*, wallflowers and salvias to fill spaces among inulas, monardas, heleniums and ligularias.
Below
Nicotiana and mauve petunias are used here to 'plug' gaps in high summer.

Above
This lovely pastel-coloured border is full of roses that have been thickly interplanted with thalictrum, verbascum and valerian. These will succeed in completely covering the soil by the middle of the summer season.

Annuals, tender perennials, biennials and seasonal bulbs are also excellent temporary fillers. You can choose from daffodils, forget-me-nots, tulips, honesty and comfrey to fill awkward spaces in the spring. In summer, cosmos, hollyhocks, agapanthus, nicotiana, cleome, alliums and amaranthus provide a tall planting mass. A selection of smaller fillers include petunias, pansies, poppies and snapdragons (*Antirrhinum*) that will remain effectively lush until they are hit by the cold.

In the maturing garden some of the primary plants will also need replacing. If these plants are identified early enough, then you will be able to replace them systematically over a period of years. This means that any unsightly gaps can be temporarily filled while the new young shrubs become established. Clearly gardens are always in a state of flux but this is all part of the fun. Simply bear in mind that when mixing shrubs with perennials you need to be highly vigilant and separate them at the first sign of hostility.

Relative Sizes This country flower garden is part of a five-acre site. This means that the plants have ample space to develop their natural habit. While waiting for the bed to mature it can be temporarily filled in the first summer with tender perennials, biennials or annuals with different forms, textures and colours to achieve a surprisingly early look of maturity.

The foundation shrubs including the evergreen *Photinia* x *fraseri*, fragrant *Philadelphus* 'Belle Etoile' and small grey-leaved *Lavandula angusti-folia* 'Hidcote' remain quite small in the first year. The *Robinia pseudoacacia* 'Frisia' will take some years to establish but the golden foliage is distinctive at an early age, changing from butter yellow in late spring to lime during the summer, then intensifying to golden rust in the autumn.

The rest of the permanent plants are herbaceous. Perpendicular rhythms of kniphofia, sisyrinchium and lavender flowers gradually assume greater importance but until then quick-fix structural plants emulate the intended look of the bed. Until the delphiniums and thalictrum fill out, you can create a well-filled look by choosing tall plants that add instant solidity. These include self-seeding perennial hollyhocks (*Alcea rosea*), which reach over 1.5 m (5 ft) in one season. For fast results they should be sown from seed in late winter for planting out in early summer after the frosts.

Echoing the vertical forms at a lower level is the fast-growing perennial *Salvia farinacea* 'Victoria' that lasts through summer. The hairy stems of the upright spider flower (*Cleome hassleriana*) are surmounted by a distinguished, rounded flower head from which emerge fine, long stamens.

While the nepeta, santolina, achillea and anthemis are growing, plants such as the white-flowered *Cosmos atrosanguineus* are used to supply the patterns and shapes of the border. The colour scheme is based on primrose- and lemon-yellows with pale blues and white. The bright green cosmos leaves blend with the feathery foliage of cream *Argyranthemum* 'Jamaica Primrose' whose daisy-like flowers create flattened shapes while the half-hardy *Osteospermum* 'Buttermilk' also works in beautifully.

First summer, above right In the first summer massed drifts of colour are quickly provided by violas while the main plants become established. The scented summer flowers of *Viola cornuta* Alba Group are pansy-faced while the true pansy *V. wittrockiana* 'Azure Blue' covers the soil. Although pansies are usually associated with spring they will flower into the summer if dead-headed. Their pale blue colour is picked up by the blue flowers of *Geranium wallichianum* 'Buxton's 'Variety' that drift among the other plants. Pale blue perennial flax (*Linum perenne*) has also been included but requires little attention.

First Summer

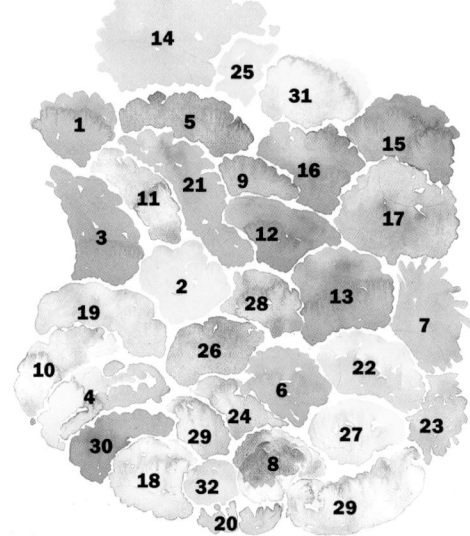

KEY *(H = Height; S = Spread)*

1. *Aconitum carmichaelii* 'Arendsii' *H: 1.5 m (5 ft); S: 30 cm (1 ft)*
2. *Achillea* 'Coronation Gold', *H: 90 cm (3 ft); S: 60 cm (2 ft)*
3. *Achillea ageratum* 'W. B. Childs', *H and S: 60 cm (2 ft)*
4. *Anthemis tinctoria* 'E. C. Buxton', *H and S: 90 cm (3 ft)*
5. *Delphinium* 'David's Magnificent', *H: 2.2 m (7 ft)*
6. *Tanacetum parthenium* 'Flore Pleno', *H: 30 cm (1 ft); S: 60 cm (2 ft)*
7. *Kniphofia* 'Primrose Beauty', *H: 90 cm (3 ft); S: 45 cm (1½ ft)*

Second Spring

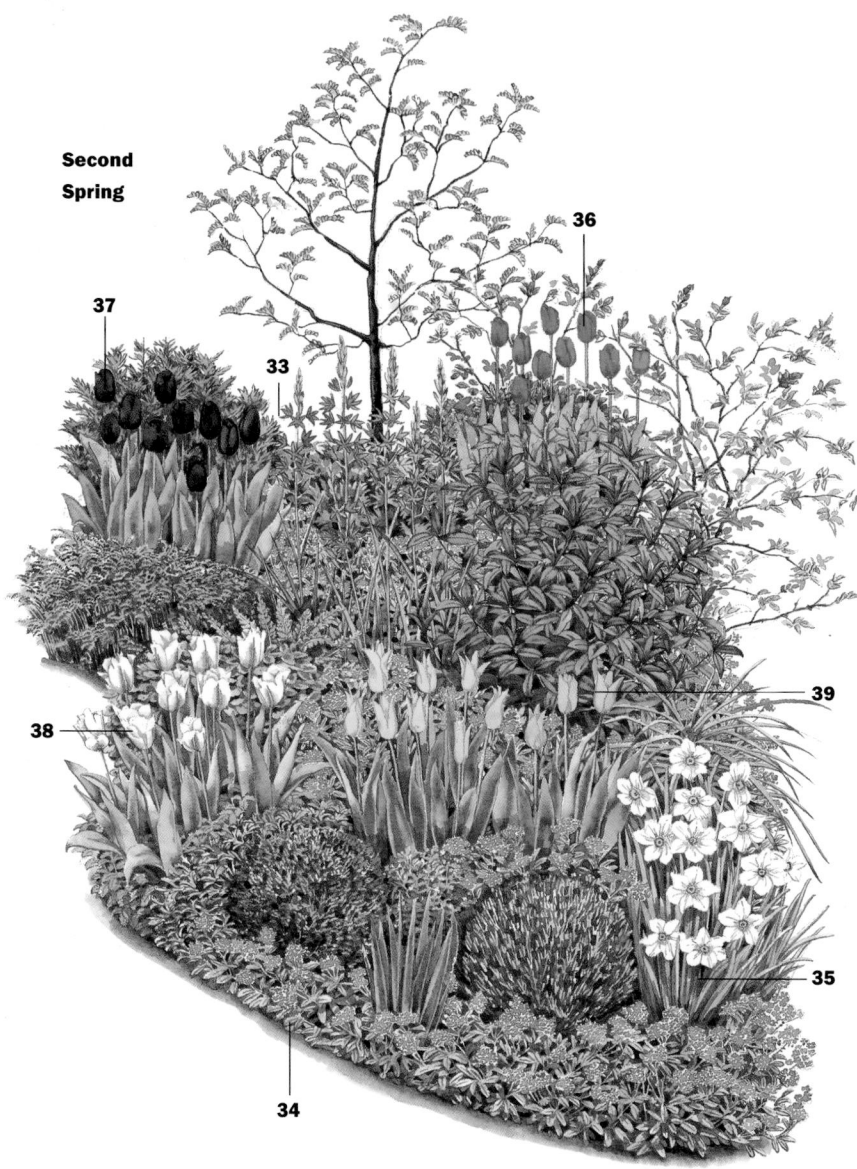

Second spring, left In the following spring, early-flowering bulbs have been planted in order to provide invaluable infilling until the summer plants become established. The tall, statuesque tulips continue the theme of rhythmical verticals and stand out among the early foliage of the many perennials. The fresh young leaves of the photinia, for example, are at their most brilliant at this time of year and are emphasized by the early red of *Tulipa* 'Couleur Cardinal'. Mid-season tulips follow amid a lavish sea of blue forget-me-nots (*Myosotis alpestris*) that echo the vibrant colour of the tall blue quamash (*Camassia cusickii*) at the back of the border. This lovely bulb has the additional advantage of lasting much longer than any of the tulip flowers.

Third summer, above By the third summer the framework shrubs are now well-established. In addition to the usual infilling of perennials and annuals other plants have been introduced into the scheme in order to vary the yearly effect including variegated *Iris pallida*, greenish-white-flowered *Nicotiana langsdorfii*, the prickly spheres of *Echinops ritro* 'Veitch's Blue', an annual pink poppy (*Papaver somniferum*) and to the right an elegant, blush-pink *Penstemon* 'Pennington Gem'.

8. *Lavandula angustifolia* 'Hidcote', *H and S:* 75 cm (2½ ft)

9. *Lychnis chalcedonica*, *H:* 90-120 cm (3-4 ft); *S:* 45 cm (1½ ft)

10. *Nepeta* 'Six Hills Giant', *H and S:* 60 cm (2 ft)

11. *Nepeta sibirica* 'Souvenir d'Andre Chaudron', *H and S:* 45 cm (1½ ft)

12. *Philadelphus* 'Belle Etoile', *H:* 1.8 m (6 ft); *S:* 1.5 m (5 ft)

13. *Photinia* x *fraseri* 'Red Robin', *H:* 6 m (20 ft); *S:* 4 m (13 ft)

14. *Robinia pseudoacacia* 'Frisia', *H:* 15 m (50 ft); *S:* 7 m (23 ft)

15. *Rosa* 'Danse du Feu', *H and S:* 2.5 m (8 ft)

16. *Rosa* 'Schoolgirl', *H:* 2.7 m (9 ft); *S:* 2.2 m (7 ft)

17. *Rosa glauca*, *H:* 1.8 m (6 ft); *S:* 1.5 m (5 ft)

18. *Santolina pinnata neapolitana*, *H:* 75 cm (2½ ft); *S:* 90 cm (3 ft)

19. *Sedum spectabile* 'Brilliant', *H and S:* 30-45 cm (1-1½ ft)

20. *Sisyrinchium striatum*, *H:* 45-60 cm (1½-2 ft); *S:* 30 cm (1 ft)

21. *Cosmos atrosanguineus*, *H:* 60 cm (2 ft); *S:* 45 cm (1½ ft)

22. *Argyranthemum* 'Jamaica Primrose', *H and S:* 90 cm (3 ft)

23. *Cleome hassleriana*, *H:* 1.2 m (4 ft); *S:* 45 cm (1½ ft)

24. *Geranium wallichianum* 'Buxton's Variety', *H:* 30-45 cm (1-1½ft); *S:* 90 cm (3 ft)

25. *Alcea rosea*, *H:* 1.5-1.8 m (5-6 ft); *S:* 60 cm (2 ft)

26. *Linum narbonense*, *H:* 30-60 cm (1-2 ft); *S:* 30 cm (1 ft)

27. *Osteospermum* 'Buttermilk', *H:* 60 cm (2 ft); *S:* 30 cm (1 ft)

28. *Salvia farinacea* 'Victoria', *H:* 90 cm (3 ft); *S:* 30 cm (1 ft)

29. *Viola* x *wittrockiana* 'Azure Blue', *H:* 15-20 cm (6-8 in); *S:* 20 cm (8 in)

30. *Viola cornuta* Alba Group, *H:* 12-20 cm (5-8 in); *S:* 20 cm (8 in)

31. *Thalictrum flavum glaucum*, *H:* 1.2-1.5 m (4-5 ft); 60 cm (2 ft)

32. *Calamintha nepeta nepeta*, *H:* 45-60 cm (1½-2 ft); *S:* 60-90 cm (2-3 ft)

33. *Camassia cusickii*, *H:* 20-80 cm (8-32 in); *S:* 20-30 cm (8-12 in)

34 *Myosotis alpestris*, *H and S:* 20 cm (8 in)

35. *Narcissus poeticus recurvus*, *H:* 42 cm (17 in)

36. *Tulipa* 'Couleur Cardinal', *H:* 60 cm (2 ft)

37. *Tulipa* 'Queen of Night', *H:* 60 cm (2 ft)

38. *Tulipa* 'Spring Green', *H:* 35-38 cm (14-15 in)

39. *Tulipa* 'West Point', *H:* 50 cm (20 in)

SUCCESSIONAL PLANTING

Gardening calls for sensitive orchestration and we can derive pleasure from organising plants to provide seasonal charm. Each plant has a moment of glory and by overlapping these the garden always holds interest. Rather like dominoes, the masquerade changes and we can plan for this.

Plants respond to day length and early in the year many plants are adapted to the shorter days. Day length changes with the seasons as is shown by the differences in plant viability. For example, plants in the tropics are more continuous while

evergreens provide a year-round background in other areas. Other plants have dormant periods although they do not awaken at the same time.

Spring is the start of the year, not January. Early eranthus, galanthus and narcissus bulbs are a promise of the future while herbaceous plants like hellebores, brunneras and bergenias accompany early flowering forsythias, daphnes, witch hazels, camellias and the Japanese quince (*Chaenomeles japonica*). *Magnolia grandiflora* 'Edith Bogue' will continue to flower intermittently after the first flush of spring. Continuity like this is invaluable. Spring reaches a climax when flowering trees such as cherries, malus and sorbus are underplanted with dicentras, wallflowers, pulsatillas, primulas and doronicums. The continuous flowering of narcissi and tulips, epimediums and *Euphorbia robbiae* then lead to early summer.

In countries like the United States, summer can vary. Some states have long summers while in others, after a period of blazing heat, all goes quiet until a 'second' summer just before the autumn. But in most areas summer produces a succession of flowering plants through early, mid-

Top left

Early schemes usually include welcome daffodils planted with tulips and forget-me-nots (*Myosotis*).

Below left

The foxtail lily (*Eremurus*) has grown very tall by summer while the flowers of *Iris* 'Flying Squadron' and *I. pallida* 'Variegata' are soon over although their leaves remain decorative for longer.

Below

This border is shown at its best with tall, pale blue delphiniums towering over spiky, dark purple salvias. The planting scheme also contains roses such as *Rosa* 'La Ville de Bruxelles' which is accompanied by *Dianthus* 'Laced Monarch' and the elegant grass *Stipa barbata*.

and late summer. At first flowering shrubs dominate the garden scene. Rhododendrons are the focus in acidic soils while elsewhere buddlejas, laburnums, peonies, lilacs and weigelas are closely followed by choisyas, cistus, deutzias and philadelphus. Herbaceous plants gather apace as the weather and soil warm up. *Myosotis* and aquilegia give way to alchemilla, gypsophila, delphiniums, lupins, dianthus, and poppies. Various forms of geranium, campanula, allium, iris and shasta daisy (*Leucanthemum* x *superbum*) can be used to stretch the flowering period further.

Above
This *Parthenocissus* is the perfect bronzed-orange foil for *Dendranthema* 'Cottage Apricot'.
Right
Annual *Salvia viridis* blend well with silver eryngiums, pink dahlias and red pelargoniums.
Below right
A late *Dahlia* 'Bishop of Llandaff' looks plush-red.

Wistaria flowers in early summer overlap with lavish *Clematis montana*. Like flowering bulbs, there is a flowering clematis for every season, from the winter-flowering *C. cirrhosa balearica* to the spring-flowering *C. alpina* and the summer-flowering 'dinner-plate' cultivars such as white *C.* 'Marie Boissellot' or *C.* 'Jackmanii Superba', and finally onto the late summer *C. viticella* group. Climbing roses also account for extended flowering periods. On the whole, ramblers have a one-off flourish while many climbers can flower twice, each time with a strong showing of flowers.

By mid-summer roses take precedence in the garden. They are as important to their time as the rhododendrons are to theirs. Footed by nepetas, alchemillas, irises or lavenders, they look magnificent. The large-flowered hybrids produce flowers for much of the season as long as they are dead-headed. Original species such as grey-leaved *R. glauca* and *R. x odorata* 'Mutabilis' with its subtle changes of colour, also have much to offer. Modern breeding practices are geared to life today which means that continuous flowering is combined with the charming natural habit, flower shape, fragrance, foliage variety and hips of old rose varieties. The apricot-yellow *R.* 'Graham Thomas' and the shell-pink *R.* 'Heritage' are good examples. There are also 'patio' or 'landscape' roses that flower for months in small gardens.

By mid- to late summer, there are fewer flowering shrubs so when fuchsias, hibiscus and hydrangeas begin to show they are very welcome. With perennials and annuals such as phlox, delphiniums, alstroemerias, anthemis, lilies, cosmos, helianthus, crocosmias, nicotiana, nigella, sidalcea, salvias, solidago and verbascums they bring form, texture and colour to the garden.

Later in the summer, when many flowers are over, biennials such as caper spurge (*Euphorbia lathyris*), mullein (*Verbascum olympicum*) and *Salvia sclarea turkestanica* are ideal for filling in gaps and covering up bare earth. Later still come agapanthus, aconites, heleniums, rudbeckias, penstemons, cimicifugas and the very late kaffir lilies (*Schizostylis*). Asters and dahlias give a heroic end-of-year performance as do *Phygelius aequalis* and *Verbena bonariensis*. However these should really be taken in for winter or thickly covered with mulch.

In autumn, azaleas, euonymus, fothergillas, parrotias, vines and acers provide a glorious finish. The red hips of roses, the bright berries of pyracantha and cotoneaster and the purple fruits of *Callicarpa bodinieri* bring added colour. Bulbs such as cyclamen, gentians, colchicums and nerines provide a far quieter note while this is also the time for frosted seed-heads and dead foliage as well as the polished beauties of bark.

Main picture, right
As this natural-looking garden shows spring planting need not be dominated by daffodils but can be filled with the subtle greenish-lilac or gentle pink colours of varieties of hellebores.
Inset, right
Pink hellebores and small white snowdrops are welcome indications of approaching spring.

A Three Season Garden This planting scheme in a shaded ditch is part of a famous garden in England designed by Margery Fish which is now being carefully maintained by the current owners. The garden has now been established for fifty years and was always intended to provide an informal part of the garden with natural-looking drifts of wild flowers and bulbs intermingled with compatible ornamental plants. Although the ditch has now dried out (probably because a well was dug locally) the soil has remained damp and at times trickles of water still supplement the muddy base.

The base of this banked ditch is composed of clay and the soil is also neutral to alkaline. The natural leaf mulch provided by the canopy of three willow trees tends to increase the levels of acidity. The top of the bank is sunnier and much drier in contrast to the damp, almost dank, lower part of the ditch. This means that plants that prefer drier conditions, such as daffodils, can be successfully grown there. The pollarded willows, which seem to oversee the entire planting scheme, also influence the success of the planting beneath them. In the spring, before the tree canopy develops fully there is,

Early spring, left and below left While the main flower displays of the summer and autumn are still to make their appearance, the ditch garden is enlivened by the foliage of geraniums, iris and bluebells. The main flowering mass at this time comes from snowdrops (*Galanthus nivalis*) that flow in dense drifts of white. These small bulbs, with strap-like leaves and elegant, bell-shaped flowers, appear in late winter and early spring, revelling in the moist, shady conditions beneath the willow trees. Other early flowers that are just starting to show through at this time of year are the perennial hellebores and lungworts (*Pulmonaria*) grown for their white or purple flowers.

Late Spring

Late spring, right The bluebell season is now at its height. Drifts of blue English bluebells (*Hyacinthoides non-scripta*) have now replaced the massed drifts of white snowdrops. Some of the geraniums are in flower and the deep, nearly black, maroon of *Geranium phaeum* flowers on the bank. Higher up, where there is more light, *G. malviflorum* has larger and paler flowers of violet-blue. The distinctive white marbling on the upper surface of the arum leaves is echoed by summer snowflakes (*Leucojum aestivum*), an early bulb with bell-shaped, green-tipped, white flowers. Solomon's seal (*Polygonatum biflorum*, syn. *P. giganteum*) also has white flowers while the flowers of *Narcissus poeticus recurvus* and *N.* 'Thalia' have all but faded. The colour scheme is, however, enlivened by yellow flag irises (*Iris pseudacorus*) and the lovely lime-green flowers of *Euphorbia amygdaloides robbiae*. These serve to complement the reddish-brown foliage of the epimediums.

of course, sufficient light to sustain the plants but as the seasons progress and the density of the tree canopy gradually increases, the levels of light are reduced and the whole look of the garden changes. This means that a succession of different plants will thrive in the ditch area according to the time of year and the light that is available. But by carefully exploiting this ever-changing natural scene, you will be able to create a constantly evolving planting scheme that stretches from early spring to late winter. These seasonal effects will overlap each other to provide continuous flowering interest.

The bank is rather steep in parts and so rocks have been inserted in order to retain the soil and to provide natural planting pockets. Many of the plants, such as the ferns, trailing ivy and epimediums, are evergreen which means that they provide the garden with a strong foundation of foliage throughout the year. The succession of seasonal flowers then appear among these permanent plants. The evergreen Gladwin iris (*Iris foetidissima*), which prefers to grow in boggy conditions, is a rhizomatous, bearded iris with dramatic, yellow-tinged, purple flowers. This iris has the added advantage of

KEY *(H = Height; S = Spread)*

Foliage Plants

1. *Asplenium scolopendrium*, H: 45-75 cm (1½-2½ ft); S: 45 cm (1½ ft)

2. *Hedera helix*, H: 10 m (30 ft); S: 5 m (15 ft)

3. *Polystichum aculeatum*, H: 60 cm (2 ft); S: 75 cm (2½ ft)

Late Spring-Flowering Plants

4. *Hyacinthoides non-scripta*, H: 20-40 cm (8-16 in); S: 8-10 cm (3-4 in)

5. *Narcissus* 'Thalia', H: 38 cm (15 in)

6. *Narcissus poeticus recurvus*, H: 42 cm (17 in)

7. *Helleborus orientalis*, H and S: 45 cm (1½ ft)

8. *Epimedium x rubrum*, H: 30 cm (1 ft); S: 20 cm (8 in)

9. *Polygonatum biflorum*, H: 1.5 m (5 ft); S: 60 cm (2 ft)

10. *Arum italicum* 'Pictum', H: 15-25 cm (6-10 in); S: 20-30 cm (8-12 in)

11. *Iris pseudacorus*, H: 1.8 m (6 ft); S: indefinite

12. *Iris foetidissima*, H: 30-90 cm (1-3 ft); S: indefinite

13. *Leucojum aestivum*, H: 50-100 cm (20-39 in); S: 10-12 cm (4-5 in)

14. *Carex pendula*, H: 90 cm (3 ft); S: 30 cm (1 ft)

15. *Euphorbia amygdaloides robbiae*, H: 45-60 cm (1½-2 ft); S: 60 cm (2 ft)

16. *Geranium phaeum*, H: 75 cm (2½ ft); S: 45 cm (1½ ft)

17. *Geranium malviflorum*, H: 75 cm (2½ ft); S: 60 cm (2 ft)

18. *Nectaroscordum siculum*, H: 1.2 m (4 ft); S: 30-45 cm (1-1½ ft)

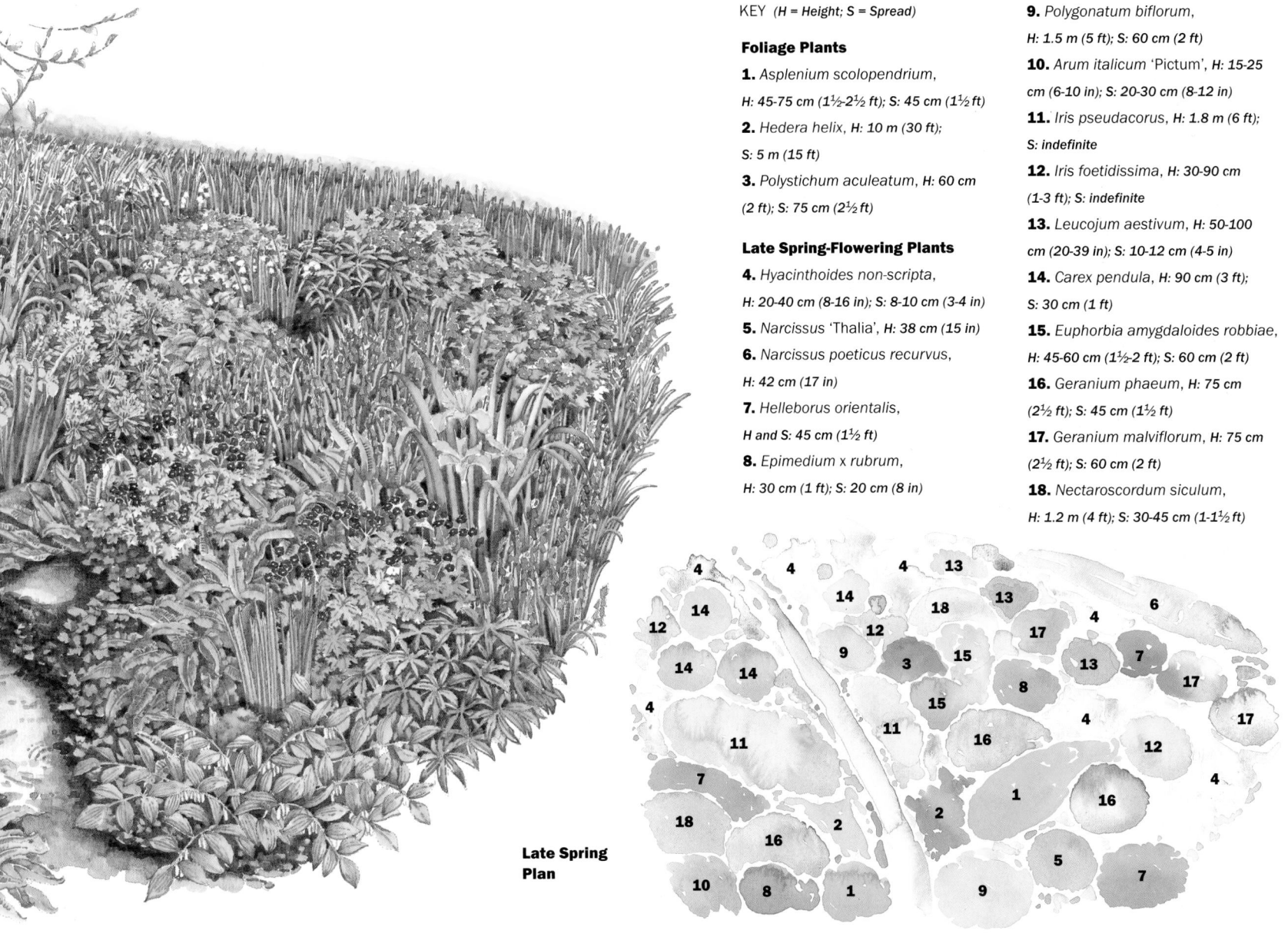

Late Spring Plan

having bright scarlet fruits throughout the winter. The leaves of the late spring-flowering *Arum italicum* 'Pictum' have striking cream or white markings on their upper surface as well as red berries in the autumn. The pendulous sedge (*Carex pendula*) is a semi-evergreen perennial with thin leaves and greenish-brown flower spikes in the summer.

Apart from these strong evergreen plants the late winter and early spring scene is dominated by snowdrops (*Galanthus nivalis*) that are densely multiplied to create white drifts that help to lift winter spirits in anticipation of the approaching spring. These bulbs are grown for their pendent, delicate, white flowers and require a partially shaded location in which to grow as well as rich, moist soil. Other flowers that are just starting to make an appearance at this time of year are the hellebores. The Christmas or Lenten rose (*Helleborus orientalis*) is ideally suited to this planting scheme, preferring shady woodland conditions and moisture-retentive but well-drained soil.

They are followed later in spring by the appearance of English bluebells (*Hyacinthoides non-scripta*) with their shining, strap-like leaves. This is the height of the bluebell season and their fragrant blue, pink or white flowers are a welcome sight at this time of year. To complement them there are also groups of daffodils within the scheme. These spring-flowering bulbs also have elegant, reed-like foliage. For example, pheasant's eye (*Narcissus poeticus recurvus*) has scented white flowers with yellow or orange centres. Additional colour is supplied by the violet-blue flowers of *Geranium malviflorum* and the black-purple flowers of *G. phaeum*.

Later in the summer, approaching the autumn, the planting changes considerably both in colour and in texture. This time of year marks the appearance of the astilbes. These hardy, late summer-flowering perennials are grown for their panicles of fluffy flowers that remain attractive even when they have dried out in the winter. This ditch garden has been planted with astilbes such as white *Astilbe* x *arendsii* 'Irrlicht' and *A. japonica* 'Red Sentinel' as well as the white, arching plumes of *A. rivularis*. The strong visual texture of these perennials contrasts strikingly with the smooth, glaucous foliage of the ferns and the perennial clump-forming hostas that make excellent ground-covers. Hostas are largely grown for their dramatic, decorative foliage. They are fully hardy and enjoy the damp, shady conditions in this garden as well as the rich, well-drained soil. There are three varieties planted in this bed including the blue-coloured *Hosta sieboldiana elegans*, which has heart-shaped, deeply ribbed leaves, *H.* 'Royal Standard' with its plain green, glossy, oval leaves and also the attractive, variegated *H. undulata albomarginata* (syn. *H.* 'Thomas Hogg').

Other valuable additions at this time of year introduce further colours to the garden. The narrow vertical perennial *Veratrum nigrum*, which is ideal for woodland gardens, has tall, elegant, chocolate-brown flower spikes and narrow, oval leaves. Its rich colour contrasts well with the white astilbes and the small, fluffy, white flowers of *Actaea alba* (syn. *A. pachypoda*). This clump-forming perennial is also blessed with white berries and scarlet stalks in the autumn which extend its season of interest still further. The evergreen

KEY *(H = Height; S = Spread)*

Late Summer/Early Autumn-Flowering Plants

19. *Astilbe* x *arendsii* 'Irrlicht', *H: 45-60 cm (1½-2ft); S: 90 cm (3 ft)*

20. *Astilbe japonica* 'Red Sentinel', *H: 60 cm (2 ft); S: 90 cm (3 ft)*

21. *Astilbe* x *arendsii* 'Snowdrift', *H: 60 cm (2 ft); S: 90 cm (3 ft)*

22. *Astilbe* x *arendsii* 'Deutschland', *H: 60 cm (2 ft); S: 90 cm (3 ft)*

23. *Astilbe* x *arendsii* 'Fanal', *H: 60 cm (2 ft); S: 90 cm (3 ft)*

24. *Astilbe rivularis*, *H: 60 cm (2 ft); S: 90 cm (3 ft)*

25. *Hosta sieboldiana elegans*, *H: 90 cm (3 ft); S: 1.5 m (5 ft)*

26. *Hosta undulata albomarginata*, *H: 75 cm (2½ ft); S: 90 cm (3 ft)*

27. *Hosta* 'Royal Standard', *H: 60 cm (2 ft); S: 1.2 m (4 ft)*

28. *Veratrum nigrum*, *H: 1.8 m (6 ft); S: 60 cm (2 ft)*

29. *Filipendula hexapetala* 'Flore Pleno', *H: 90 cm (3 ft); S: 45 cm (1½ ft)*

30. *Actaea alba*, *H: 90 cm (3 ft); S: 50 cm (20 in)*

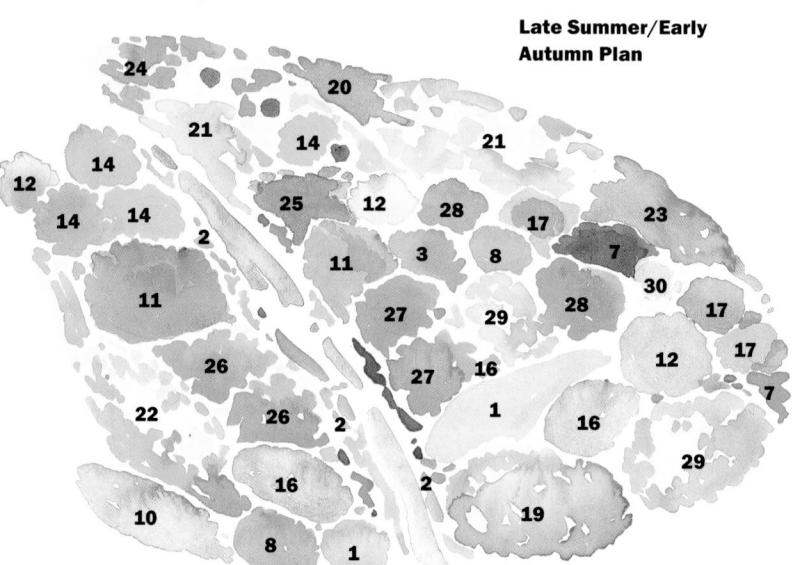

Late Summer/Early Autumn Plan

foliage of the different varieties of ferns, the ivies and the *Lysimachia num-mularia* provide year-round foliage interest. Indeed, although the flowers of the yellow flag iris (*Iris pseudacorus*), the Gladwin iris (*I. foetidissima*), the mourning widow (*Geranium phaeum*) and *G. malviflorum* have faded their leaves are still present and the cycle can start again in early spring. The foliage of the carpeting perennial *Epimedium* x *rubrum* also remains long after its crimson flowers have gone.

Late summer/early autumn, below During the same year the scene has changed considerably. Foliage still holds the scheme together with tall, green spears of flag iris, hostas overlapping in concentric layers and the pleated leaves of *Veratrum nigrum* supporting tall maroon-black flowers. But the dense willow canopy means that most of the flowers are situated on the periphery of the ditch where the light is more dappled. These include a host of fluffy flowered astilbes of varying colours massed at the border edge. The arum is now without its leaves but instead offers spiked stems of red berries while the *Iris foetidissima* has orange-red berries to provide vivid splashes of late colour.

Late Summer/Early Autumn

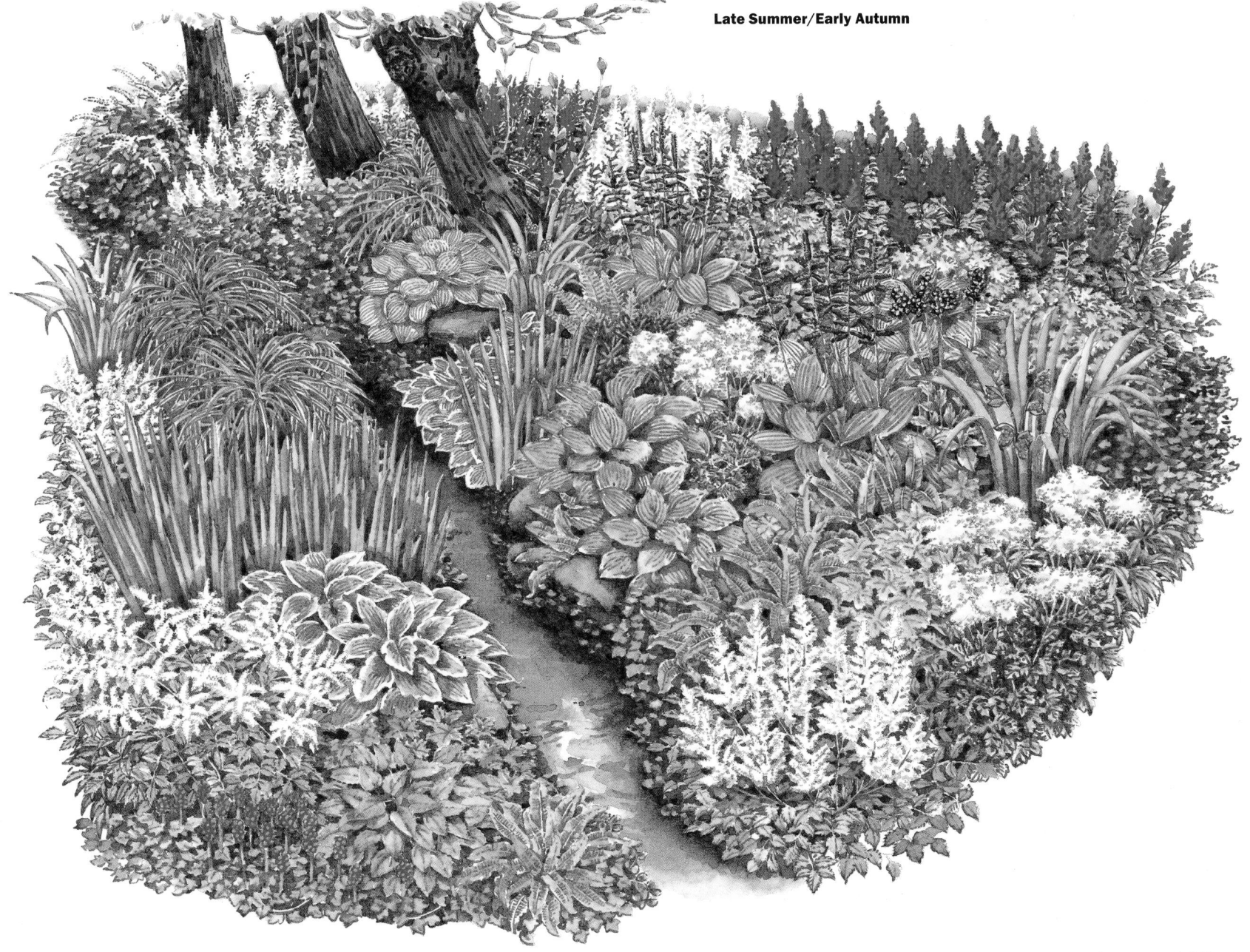

MAINTAINING HARMONY AND BALANCE

Observation is the name of the game in gardening. 'Green-fingered' people are simply observant and nurture plants so that they reach their optimum size and sometimes prune them to shape. There is an art to this: you prune to benefit the plant and improve balance, flowering and health or you prune and train to impose a structure.

Look at a plant's natural growth habit first. For example, ornamental quinces (*Chaenomeles*) are naturally elegant, branching with such style that a single specimen can be displayed with minimalist charm. The densely chaotic foliage of forsythias, however, must be cut back immediately after flowering because they flower on the previous year's wood and lack form. Many people resolve this by clipping them formally as a hedge. I have cut an old forsythia shrub to the ground because there was no structure to guide me. Therein lies the key to pruning: either you impose your will and virtually topiary a plant or you remove branches to accentuate its natural habit.

You will also have to remove eccentric growth. A shrub may have an unbalanced profile on purchase but this can be corrected through pruning. Ornamental dogwoods, such as *Cornus alba* 'Sibirica', and willows like *Salix alba vitellina* 'Britzensis' can be pruned hard in alternate years in late spring. Pruning all-green branches also prevents variegated plants such as *Buddleja davidii* 'Harlequin' from reverting. Thinning out branches also lets in light and air to improve their health. Remove old, damaged wood to prevent die-back and watch for vigour-reducing suckers.

Some shrubs can become top heavy with age, emulating the branching habit of trees. Cutting back into old wood will kill them but you can pre-vent stems from developing into untidy growth by pruning in spring. Brooms (*Cytisus*), for example, should be controlled on a yearly basis to maintain compact growth. Larger shrubs like buddlejas will outgrow the garden unless cut back each year.

Encouraging a shrub or tree to flower or fruit is one of the main reasons for pruning. Plants such as hardy fuchsias, ceratostigma, perovskia, lavateras or *Clematis* 'Jackmanii Superba' flower on the current season's growth and should be

Above
Kniphofia 'Sunningdale Yellow' and *Penstemon* 'Pennington Gem' flower once while *Anthemis tinctoria* 'E. C. Buxton' flowers again if it is clipped.
Top near right
These artemisias should be tidied after flowering while *Rosa* 'Aloha' should be pruned every year.
Top centre right
Perennials may need cutting back in autumn or spring and dividing every two to three years.
Top far right
Macleaya cordata in full flower behind *Phlox paniculata* 'Starfire' will need tidying in autumn.
Right
To achieve this summer view of roses, peonies and dianthus careful preparation starts in early spring.

hard pruned in spring of the same year. Shrubs like forsythias, deutzia, kolkwitzia and some of the large hybrid clematis flower on wood that is two or more seasons old and should have some stems cut low down immediately after flowering to encourage growth from the base. New growth will then appear during the summer upon which spring flowers will appear the following year.

Roses need pruning in different ways. 'Hybrid tea' roses or large-flowered bush roses offer the perfect specimen flower. They have a stiff, vertical growth but you can encourage a rounder habit by cutting the branches by 60-90 cm (2-3 ft) down to an outward-facing bud. This allows air to circulate easily through the centre of the shrub. Old shrub roses are different. Many are very tall with a lax habit. Their flowers are followed by hips, and should be pruned minimally by thinning out the shrub removing old, dead wood.

Old roses such as *Rosa moyesii*, *R*. glauca, albas, damasks, bourbons and rugosas have all-round personalities with foliage, habit, fragrance and fruit to recommend them as well as flowers. Many of these characteristics are missing from some of the large-flowered roses but recent hybridizing has explored these qualities and new varieties of shrub roses including apricot *R*. 'Abraham Darby' and pale *R*. 'Peach Blossom' are now available. These fragrant 'New English Roses' can also be deep red, carmine, yellow and white. Any weak growth should be removed in early spring.

Compact ornamentals such as daphnes, cistus, choisyas and myrtle will require tidying up. In general, the good health of plants such as these calls for continual care by removing competitive weeds and looking for signs of stress. Sensitive observation is what good gardening is all about.

A Three-Year Plan This beautiful border, which has been deliberately restricted to hot colours, mixes perennials with selected shrubs and aims for a lush summer look. The permanent shrubs include *Cornus alba* 'Spaethii' and two shrub roses, *Rosa moyesii* 'Geranium' and *Rosa* 'Chinatown which work particularly well with the perennial scheme. Group planting of herbaceous perennials starts the border off but it will take approximately three years for the plants to grow to their full height and spread. In the meantime, annuals and tender perennials can provide an almost instant effect.

Red flowers are the perfect way of maintaining a hot summer look. Tender antirrhinums, pelargoniums, lobelias and penstemons are chosen with this in mind. The unique love-lies-bleeding (*Amaranthus communis* 'Peeping Tom') has pendulous panicles of velvety red flowers trailing from bushy, light green foliage. Adding depth of colour and height the striking cannas have bronzed leaves upon which tall stems of cardinal-red flowers are held. Though truly perennial they are planted out annually. A number of fast-growing red orach (*Atriplex hortensis rubra*) have also been planted to balance the dark canna foliage. The castor oil plant (*Ricinus communis*) provides an exotic pattern with its dramatic leaves while the equally distinctive ruby chard (*Beta vulgaris cicla*) has scarlet stems from which large green leaves emerge. To extend the season still further dahlias such as *Dahlia* 'Bishop of Llandaff' will survive modest winters and co-operate well with the bottle hips of the species rose as autumn approaches.

KEY *(H = Height; S= Spread)*

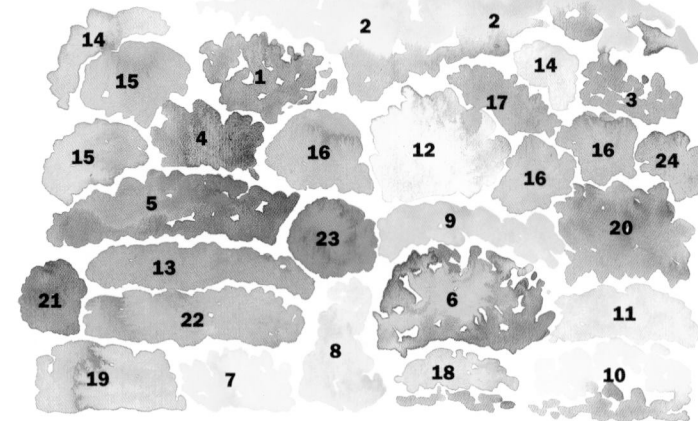

1. *Rosa moyesii* 'Geranium', *H: 3 m (10 ft); S: 2.5 m (8 ft)*

2. *Rudbeckia laciniata*, *H: 1.8-2.2 m (6-7 ft); S: 60-90 cm (2-3 ft)*

3. *Rosa* 'Chinatown', *H: 3 m (10 ft); S: 2.5 m (8 ft)*

4. *Atriplex hortensis rubra*, *H: 1.2 m (4 ft); S: 30 cm (1 ft)*

5. *Crocosmia* 'Lucifer', *H: 90 cm (3 ft); S: 20-25 cm (8-10 in)*

6. *Crocosmia masionorum*, *H: 1.5 m (5 ft); S: 30-45 cm (1-1½ ft)*

7. *Coreopsis verticillata* 'Moonbeam', *H: 40-60 cm (16-24 in); S: 30 cm (1 ft)*

8. *Solidago* 'Crown of Rays', *H: 75 cm (2½ ft); S: 45 cm (1½ ft)*

9. *Achillea filipendulina* 'Gold Plate', *H: 1.2 m (4 ft); S: 60 cm (2 ft)*

10. *Helenium* 'Butterpat', *H: 90 cm (3 ft); S: 60 cm (2 ft)*

11. *Helenium* 'Moerheim Beauty', *H: 90 cm (3 ft); S: 60 cm (2 ft)*

12. *Cornus alba* 'Spaethii', *H: 2.2 m (7 ft); S: 1.8 m (6 ft)*

13. *Amaranthus caudatus*, *H: 1.2 m (4 ft); S: 45 cm (1½ ft)*

14. *Canna x generalis*, *H: 1.2 m (4 ft); S: 45-60 cm (1- 1½ ft)*

15. *Dahlia* 'Bishop of Llandaff', *H and S: 90 cm (3 ft)*

16. *Dahlia* 'Blaisdon Red', *H and S: 90 cm (3 ft)*

17. *Lobelia cardinalis*, *H: 90 cm (3 ft); S: 23 cm (9 in)*

18. *Penstemon* 'Garnet', *H: 60-75 cm (2-2½ ft); S: 60 cm (2 ft)*

19. *Antirrhinum* (red), *H: 60-75 cm (2-2½ ft); S: 45 cm (1½ ft)*

20. *Ricinus communis*, *H: 1.5 m (5 ft); S: 90 cm (3 ft)*

21. *Beta vulgaris cicla*, *H: 60 cm (2 ft); S: 45 cm (1½ ft)*

22. *Pelargonium x hortorum*, *H: 60 cm (2 ft); S: 45 cm (1½ ft)*

23. *Pelargonium* 'Madame Butterfly', *H: 60-75 cm (2-2½ ft); S: 45 cm (1½ ft)*

24. *Antirrhinum* 'Black Prince', *H: 60-75 cm (2-2½ ft); S: 45 cm (1½ ft)*

25. *Lobelia* 'Queen Victoria', *H: 90 cm (3 ft); S: 30 cm (1 ft)*

26. *Penstemon* 'Firebird', *H: 60-75 cm (2-2½ ft); S: 60 cm (2 ft)*

27. *Petunia x hybrida* (red), *H: 15-30 cm (6-12 in); S: 30 cm (1 ft)*

First summer, below In the first summer the permanent shrubs and herbaceous perennials are not yet fully established. They have been interplanted with colourful annuals and perennials which means that gaps in the planting are less noticeable. The red, yellow and orange colour scheme is, however, apparent and gives a hint of the border's final impact.

First Summer

Second summer, right By the following summer many of the perennials are filling out. The small *Coreopsis verticillata* 'Moonbeam' that edges the border is wider; the *Solidago* 'Crown of Rays' is spreading; both the crocosmias are increasing in mass; and *Helenium* 'Butterpat' and *H*. 'Moerheim Beauty' are also starting to spread out. The annual *Atriplex hortensis rubra* has also self-seeded. The permanent shrubs have settled in well but the perennials are still needed to cover the patches of bare earth between them while they grow. Although the lobelia, cannas, ricinus and the amaranthus are still used, they become less evident as the main plants start to dominate the border. However, red petunias, penstemons and pelargoniums are still used as infillers.

Second Summer

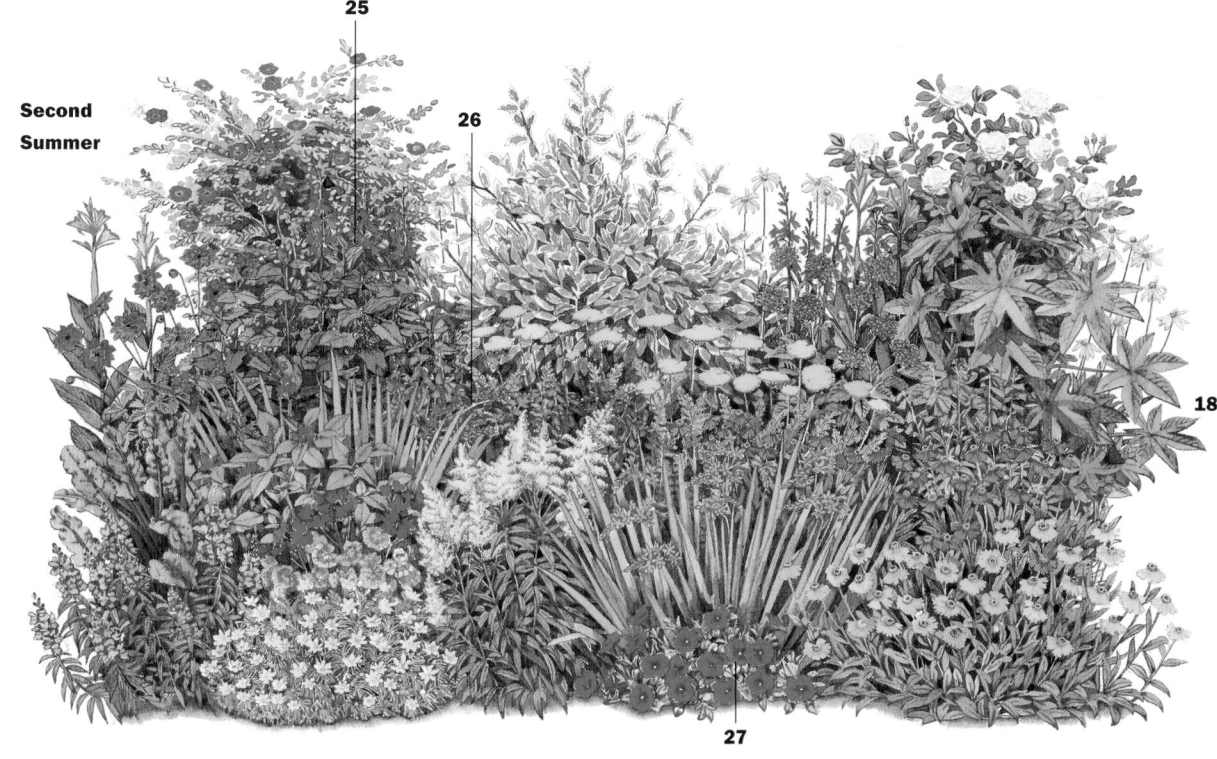

Third summer, above The main shrubs are nearing their final size. The border has filled out with the permanent herbaceous plants also starting to dominate. The tall crocosmias and the sneezeweeds (*Helenium*) are naturally clumped and are very influential and will eventually need dividing as they become more congested. *Achillea filipendulina* 'Gold Plate' has drifted across the border with its golden, flat-headed flowers. Dahlias are again included for a late season colour display but now the gaps between the herbaceous perennials are completely filled in.

153

A Five-Year Plan We all need our own space and as vegetation is not mobile gardeners need to allow the plants room to grow in comfort so that they can display their natural shapes. Often, in small gardens, this denies us as much choice as we would like and there is a tendency to simply 'stuff' the plants in. I have done this myself, eager to cover up every area of bare soil. A sensitive planting scheme, however, should acknowledge the passage of time and allow each plant to reach its full height and spread. To do this you need to know the final size of each individual plant before you start and space the young plants at correct intervals. This is not always easy to achieve when you are eager to create a bed or border. It is tempting to go for instant effects and sometimes, looking at the young specimen, it is difficult to appreciate how large it will eventually become.

Year One

Year three, below By the third summer the permanent shrubs are beginning to fill out the bed. The two conifers, in particular, make an increasingly important mark as they grow. However, the *Acer davidii* will create a wide canopy and affect the plants beneath unless it is cut back. Beneath the shrubs many of the herbaceous plants are also expanding. For example, the variegated *Euphorbia characias wulfenii* will eventually become a large mound while mats of purple sage (*Salvia officinalis* Purpurascens Group), flowering *Osteospermum* 'Silver Sparkler' and the scented *Sedum populifolium* will gradually fill out the border edge.

Year one, above Within the basic framework of evergreen and deciduous shrubs a variety of herbaceous perennials have been planted in order to bring early colour until the main plants become fully established. After the first twelve months have passed the perennials are beginning to become established themselves including the upright foxglove (*Digitalis grandiflora*). The narrow vertical perennial *Kniphofia* 'Percy's Pride' is striking with its green-tinged, yellow flower spikes as are the daylily *Hemerocallis* 'Whichford' and the feathery plumes of the *Macleaya cordata*. Echoing this strongly upright pattern beneath them are plants that have grass-like foliage. These include the lilyturf (*Liriope muscari*), a spreading perennial with lavender or purple bell-shaped flowers and glossy, strap-like leaves. The Gladwin iris (*Iris foetidissima*) and *Elymus hispidus* with its rather elegant, steel-blue leaves are also noticeable at this time. The pink meadow cranesbill, *Geranium pratense* 'Mrs Kendall Clark', and the lilac blue *Aster thomsonii* 'Nanus' will contribute more to the bed as the years pass.

Year Three

In this sunny mixed border the scale of shrubs has been carefully considered in relation to the other herbaceous plants. At the back of the bed, establishing a framework for the future, a foundation of evergreen shrubs has been planted including the variegated holly (*Ilex aquifolium* 'Aureamarginata'), the glossy-leaved common laurel (*Prunus laurocerasus*) and the fragrant sweet box (*Sarcococca confusa*). At either end of the border the narrowly vertical yews (*Taxus baccata* 'Fastigiata') contain the whole group. Some deciduous shrubs, such as the bronzed-pink *Cotinus obovatus*, which flares up magnificently in the autumn, the purple-grey foliage of *Rosa glauca* (syn. *R. rubrifolia*) , the red-stemmed dogwood (*Cornus alba* 'Elegantissima') and the ever-silver *Brachyglottis compacta* 'Sunshine' with its yellow daisy-like summer flowers, add colourful foliage to the scheme.

KEY *(H = Height; S= Spread)*

1. *Escallonia* 'Iveyi', *H and S: 3 m (10 ft)*

2. *Cotinus obovatus*, *H: 10 m (30 ft); S: 8 m (25 ft)*

3. *Ilex aquifolium* 'Aureamarginata', *H: 14 m (46 ft); S: 5 m (15 ft)*

4. *Prunus laurocerasus* 'Castlewellan', *H: 6 m (20 ft); S: 10 m (30 ft)*

5. *Acer davidii*, *H and S: 15 m (50 ft)*

6. *Taxus baccata* 'Fastigiata', *H: 10-15 m (30-50 ft); S: 5-10 m (15-30 ft)*

7. *Cornus alba* 'Elegantissima', *H and S: 1.5 m (5 ft)*

8. *Rosa glauca*, *H: 1.8 m (6 ft); S: 1.5 m (5 ft)*

9. *Sarcococca confusa*, *H and S: 90 cm (3 ft)*

10. *Digitalis grandiflora*, *H: 75 cm (2½ ft); S: 30 cm (1 ft)*

11. *Viola cornuta*, *H: 12-20 cm (5-8 in); S: 20 cm (8 in)*

12. *Elymus hispidus*, *H: 90 cm (3 ft); S: 60 cm (2 ft)*

13. *Hosta* 'Halcyon', *H: 30 cm (1 ft); S: 90 cm (3 ft)*

14. *Macleaya cordata*, *H: 1.5 m (5 ft); S: 60 cm (2 ft)*

15. *Euphorbia characias wulfenii* 'Burrow Silver', *H and S: 1.2 m (4 ft)*

16. *Osteospermum* 'Silver Sparkler', *H: 30 cm (1 ft); S: 45 cm (1½ ft)*

17. *Salvia officinalis* Purpurascens Group, *H: 60 cm (2 ft); S: 90 cm (3 ft)*

18. *Kniphofia* 'Percy's Pride', *H: 90 cm (3 ft); S: 50 cm (20 in)*

19. *Artemisia absinthium* 'Lambrook Silver', *H: 80 cm (32 in); S: 50 cm (20 in)*

20. *Brachyglottis compacta* 'Sunshine', *H: 90 cm (3 ft); S: 1.5 m (5 ft)*

21. *Salvia verticillata* 'Alba', *H: 60 cm (2 ft); S: 90 cm (3 ft)*

22. *Hemerocallis* 'Whichford', *H: 75 cm (2½ ft); S: 90 cm (3 ft)*

23. *Aster thomsonii* 'Nanus', *H: 45 cm (1½ ft); S: 23 cm (9 in)*

24. *Liriope muscari*, *H: 30 cm (1 ft); S: 45 cm (1½ ft)*

25. *Artemisia lactiflora* Guizhou Group, *H: 1.2-1.5 m (4-5 ft); S: 50 cm (20 in)*

26. *Euphorbia dulcis* 'Chameleon', *H and S: 1.2 m (4 ft)*

27. *Sedum populifolium*, *H: 30-45 cm (1-1½ ft); S: 30 cm (1 ft)*

28. *Euonymus fortunei* 'Emerald Gaiety', *H: 90 cm (3 ft); S: 1.5 m (5 ft)*

29. *Iris foetidissima*, *H: 30-90 cm (1-3 ft); S: indefinite*

30. *Geranium pratense* 'Mrs Kendall Clark', *H: 75 cm (2½ ft); S: 60 cm (2 ft)*

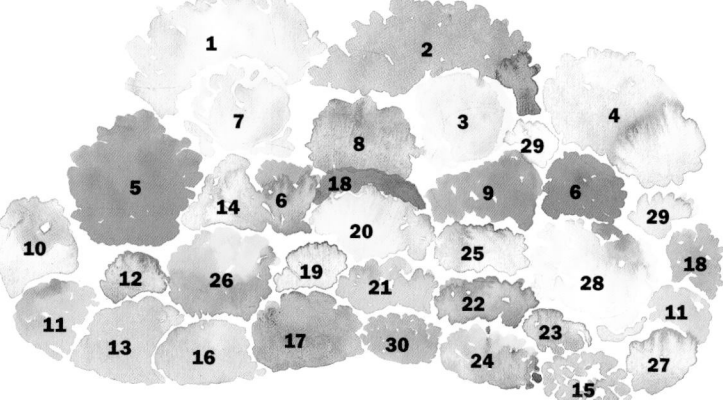

Year five, above After five years the border is now lush and fully mature. The yew tree on the left is well above head height and the other yew, although it has not made quite the same growth, is now developing well. All the shrubs are gradually encroaching on the herbaceous plants but the plume poppy (*Macleaya cordata*) will spread very rapidly unless it is controlled. In fact, there comes a point in the life of every mixed border when it is necessary to thin out the planting to some extent. Many perennials do a good job in a bed for the first five years but now may be the time to make some choices by transplanting them elsewhere.

INDEX

ACKNOWLEDGEMENTS

Clive Nichols would like to thank the following designers, garden owners and organizations for allowing photography in their gardens for this book ;

KEY: **t** = top **b** = bottom **l** = left **c** = centre **r** = right ***d*** = designer

p1 ***d.*** Piet and Anja Oudolf, Hummelo, Holland **p2-3** Bosvigo House, Truro, Cornwall ***d.*** Michael and Wendy Perry **p4-5 t.l.** Little Court, Crawley, Hants **t.c.** Coton Manor Gardens, Ravensthorpe, Northants **t.r.** Barnsley House, Barnsley, Glos **c.l.** The White House, Burpham, Sussex ***d.*** Elisabeth Woodhouse **c.r.** ***d.*** Piet and Anja Oudolf, Hummelo, Holland **b.l.** Eastgrove Cottage Garden and Nursery, Sankyns Green, Worcs **b.c.** ***d.*** Keeyla Meadows, San Francisco **b.r.** Greystone Cottage, Kingwood Common, Oxon **p6** Redenham Park, Hants ***d.*** Olivia Clarke **p7** Hadspen House Garden and Nursery, Somerset ***d.*** Sandra and Nori Pope **p8 l.** Bosvigo House, Truro, Cornwall ***d.*** Michael and Wendy Perry **p8-9** La Casella, France ***d.*** Claus Scheinert **p9 r.** Redenham Park, Hants ***d.*** Olivia Clarke **p10** The Anchorage, Kent ***d.*** Wendy Francis **p11 t.** The Old Rectory, Sudborough, Northants **b.** Greenhurst Garden, Sussex ***d.*** Gilly Hopton **p12 inset** Pro Carton Garden, Chelsea 1996 ***d.*** Julie Toll **p12-13** Benington Lordship, Herts **p13 r.** The Savill Garden, Surrey **p14** Tuinen Ton Ter Linden, Ruinen, Holland **p15 l.** ***d.*** Piet and Anja Oudolf, Hummelo, Holland **t.** ***d.*** Piet and Anja Oudolf, Hummelo, Holland **p16 t.** Feibusch Garden, San Francisco **b.** ***d.*** Sarah Hammond, California **p17** ***d.*** Gordon White, Austin, Texas **p18-19** The White House, Burpham, Sussex ***d.*** Elisabeth Woodhouse **p20** Bourton House, Glos **p21** Manoir Aux Quat' Saisons, Oxon **p22 l.** Barnsley House, Barnsley, Glos **r.** The White House, Burpham, Sussex ***d.*** Elisabeth Woodhouse **p23 l.** Coton Manor Gardens, Ravensthorpe, Northants **r.** White Windows, Longparish, Hants **p24 l.** ***d.*** Gordon White, Austin, Texas **r.** Huntington Botanical Gardens, Los Angeles **p25 l.** Ashtree Cottage, Wilts **r.** Strybing Arboretum, San Francisco **p26 t.** ***d*** Piet and Anja Oudolf, Hummelo, Holland **b.** Huntington Botanical Gardens, Los Angeles **p27 t.** ***d.*** Piet and Anja Oudolf, Hummelo, Holland **b.** Tuinen Ton Ter Linden, Ruinen, Holland **p28** The Old Vicarage, East Ruston, Norfolk ***d.*** Graham Robeson and Alan Gray **p29 t.** The Beth Chatto Gardens, Elmstead Market, Essex **c.** Wollerton Old Hall, Shropshire **b.** Butterstream, Trim, County Meath, Republic of Ireland **p30 l.** The White House, Burpham, Sussex ***d.*** Elisabeth Woodhouse **c.** La Casella, France ***d.*** Claus Scheinert **r.** Mottisfont Abbey, Hants **p31 l.** Bosvigo House, Truro, Cornwall ***d.*** Michael and Wendy Perry **r.** Wollerton Old Hall, Shropshire **p32 l.** Lakemount, Glanmire, County Cork, Republic of Ireland ***d.*** Brian Cross **r.** Meadow House, Wolverton Common, Berks **p33 l.** Barnsley House, Glos **r.** Wollerton Old Hall, Shropshire **p34 l.** 40, Osler Road, Oxon **c.** Ashtree Cottage, Wilts **r.** 40, Osler Road, Oxon **p35 l.** Barnsley House, Glos **r.** Mr Fraser's garden, West Sussex ***d.*** Julian Treyer-Evans **p36 t.** Tuinen Ton Ter Linden, Ruinen, Holland **b.** Wollerton Old Hall, Shropshire **p37 t.** Huntington Botanical Garden, Los Angeles **c.** Jardin Canario, Gran Canaria, Canary Islands **b.** ***d.*** Roger Raiche, San Francisco, California **p38 t.** Sticky Wicket, Dorset ***d.*** Peter and Pam Lewis **b.** ***d.*** Sarah Hammond, California **p39 t.** ***d.*** Sarah Hammond, California **b.** Huntington Botanical Garden, Los Angeles **p41** ***d.*** Sarah Hammond, California **p42** The White House, Burpham, Sussex ***d.*** Elisabeth Woodhouse **p43** Bourton House, Oxon **p44 t.** ***d.*** Sue Berger, Bristol, Avon **c.** ***d.*** Malley Terry **b.** Tuinen Ton Ter Linden, Ruinen, Holland **p45 t.** Chelsea 1994 ***d.*** Lucy Huntington **b.** Butterstream, Trim, County Meath, Republic of Ireland **p46 l.** Exbury Gardens, Hants **rt.** Ivy Cottage, Dorset **br.** North Springs, Fittleworth, West Sussex **p47 t.** Wollerton Old Hall, Shropshire **c.** Hexham Herbs, Northumberland **b.** Longacre, Kent **p48 far l.** ***d.*** Roger Raiche, San Francisco **c.l.** Strybing Arboretum, San Francisco **c.r.** Huntington Botanical Garden, Los Angeles **far r.** Butterstream, Trim, County Meath, Republic of Ireland **p49 far l.** Eastgrove Cottage Garden, Sankyns Green, Worcs ***d.*** Carol and Malcolm Skinner **c.l.** Strybing Arboretum, San Francisco **c.r.** Eastgrove Cottage Garden, Sankyns Green, Worcs ***d.*** Malcolm and Carol Skinner **far r.** ***d.*** James David, Texas **p51 c.l.** East Lambrook Manor, Somerset **b.** Huntington Botanical Garden, Los Angeles **t.c.** ***d.*** Myles Challis, London **t.r.** Feibusch Garden, San Francisco **b.r.** Copton Ash, Kent **p52 l.** ***d.*** James David, Austin Texas **c.** Mottisfont Abbey, Hants **r.** The Priory, Kemerton, Worcs **p53 l.** ***d.*** Dan Pearson **c.** ***d.*** Mark Brown, Normandy, France **r.** The Beth Chatto Gardens, Elmstead Market, Essex **p54 t.** Royal Horticultural Society's Garden, Surrey **c.** Bourton House Garden, Glos **b.** ***d.*** Roger Platts **p55** Hadspen House Garden and Nursery, Somerset ***d.*** Sandra and Nori Pope **p56 t.l.** Wollerton Old Hall, Shropshire **t.r.** Lower Hall, Worfield, Shropshire **b.** ***d.*** Piet and Anja Oudolf, Hummelo, Holland **p58 l.** Lower Hall, Worfield, Shropshire **r.** ***d.*** Suzanne Porter, San Francisco **p59 t.** Eastgrove Cottage Garden and Nursery, Sankyns Green, Worcs ***d.*** Malcolm and Carol Skinner **b.** Wollerton Old Hall, Shropshire **p60 t.** Longacre, Kent **c.** Coates Manor, Sussex **b.** University Botanic Garden, Cambridge, Camb **p61 t.** The White House, Burpham, Sussex ***d.*** Elisabeth Woodhouse **b.** The Dillon Garden, Dublin, Republic of Ireland **p62 l.** Mr Fraser's garden, West Sussex ***d.*** Julian Treyer-Evans **c.** Copton Ash, Kent **r.** Mr Fraser's garden, West Sussex ***d.*** Julian Treyer-Evans **p63 l.** Mr Fraser's garden, West Sussex ***d.*** Julian Treyer-Evans **c.** Hadspen House Garden and Nursery, Somerset ***d.*** Sandra and Nori Pope **r.** Coton Manor Gardens, Ravensthorpe, Northants **p65** The Old Vicarage, East Ruston, Norfolk ***d.*** Graham Robeson and Alan Gray **p66** The Dillon Garden, Dublin, Republic of Ireland **p67** The Dillon Garden, Dublin, Republic of Ireland **p68 l.** The White House, Burpham, Sussex ***d.*** Elisabeth Woodhouse **c.** Chenies Manor Garden, Bucks **r.** Feibusch Garden, San Francisco **p69** Little Coopers, Eversley, Hants **p70 t.** White Windows, Longparish, Hants **b.** Leonardslee Gardens, Handcross, Sussex **p71 l.** The Old Rectory, Tidmarsh, Berks **r.** ***d.*** Sheila Jackson, London **p72 t.** ***d.*** Piet and Anja Oudolf, Hummelo, Holland **b.** ***d.*** Piet and Anja Oudolf, Hummelo, Holland **p73 t.l.** Coton Manor Gardens, Ravensthorpe, Northants **tr.** Coton Manor Gardens, Ravensthorpe, Northants **b.l.** Chenies Manor Garden, Bucks **b.r.** Bosvigo House, Truro, Cornwall ***d.*** Wendy and Michael Perry **p74** Herterton House Garden, Cambo, Morpeth, Northumberland **p75 l.** Bosvigo House, Truro, Cornwall ***d.*** Wendy and Michael Perry **r.** The Priory, Kemerton, Worcs **p76 t.** ***d.*** Piet and Anja Oudolf, Hummelo, Holland **c.** Sleightholme Dale Lodge, Fadmoor, North Yorkshire **b.** ***d.*** Piet and Anja Oudolf, Hummelo, Holland **p77 t.l.** Little Coopers, Eversley, Hants **r.** Eastgrove Cottage Garden and Nursery, Sankyns Green, Worcs **b.** Bourton House, Oxon **p78 t.** Coates Manor, Sussex **b.** Tuinen Ton Ter Linden, Ruinen, Holland **p79 l.** The White House, Burpham, Sussex ***d.*** Elisabeth Woodhouse **c.** The Dillon Garden, Dublin, Republic of Ireland **r.** Barnsley House, Glos **p80** Wollerton Old Hall, Shropshire **p81 t.l.** The Telegraph Garden, Chelsea 1995 ***d.*** Arabella Lennox-Boyd **t.r.** Chenies Manor Garden, Bucks **b.l.** Chenies Manor Garden, Bucks **p81 br.** ***d.*** Olivia Clarke **p82** Chenies Manor Garden, Bucks **p85 t.l.** Wollerton Old Hall, Shropshire **b.l.** Tuinen Ton Ter Linden, Ruinen, Holland **t.r.** Meadow House, Wolverton Common, Berks **c.r.** The Beth Chatto Gardens, Elmstead Market, Essex **b.r.** Herterton House Garden, Cambo, Morpeth, Northumberland **p86 t.r.** Wollerton Old Hall, Shropshire **t.c.** Little Coopers, Eversley, Hants **t.r.** Strybing Arboretum, San Francisco **c.l.** The Priory, Kemerton, Worcs **c.c.** Chenies Manor Garden, Bucks **c.r.** Wollerton Old Hall, Shropshire **bl.** Lakemount, Glanmire, County Cork, Republic of Ireland **b.c.** Hadspen House Garden and Nursery, Somerset ***d.*** Sandra and Nori Pope **b.r.** The Dillon Garden, Dublin, Republic of Ireland **p88** Feibusch Garden, San Francisco **p89 t.l.** Wollerton Old Hall, Shropshire **t.r.** Coton Manor Gardens, Ravensthorpe, Northants **b.l.** Coton Manor Gardens, Ravensthorpe, Northants **b.r.** The Dillon Garden, Dublin, Republic of Ireland **p91** Coton Manor Gardens, Ravensthorpe, Northants **p93** Coton Manor Gardens, Ravensthorpe, Northants **p94 l.** Bosvigo House, Truro, Cornwall ***d.*** Michael and Wendy Perry **c.** The Priory, Kemerton, Worcs **r.** The Castle Grounds, Guildford, Surrey **p95 l.** Bosvigo House, Truro, Cornwall ***d.*** Michael and Wendy Perry **c.** Chenies Manor Garden, Bucks **r.** Royal Horticultural Society's Garden, Surrey **p96 t.** Ashtree Cottage, Wilts **c.** La Casella, France. ***d.*** Claus Scheinert **b.** Eastgrove Cottage Garden, Sankyns Green, Worcs ***d.*** Malcolm and Carol Skinner **p97 t.** Meadow House, Wolverton Common, Berks **b.** Wollerton Old Hall, Shropshire **p98 t.** The Anchorage, Kent **b.** Ashtree Cottage, Wilts **p99 l.** Eastgrove Cottage Garden, Sankyns Green, Worcs ***d.*** Malcolm and Carol Skinner **r.** The Anchorage, Kent **p101 t.l.** Bourton House, Glos **t.c.** Butterstream, Trim, County Meath, Republic of Ireland **t.r.** The Beth Chatto Gardens, Elmstead Market, Essex **c.l.** ***d.*** Lucy Huntington **c.c.** Chenies Manor Garden, Bucks **c.r.** ***d.*** Piet and Anja Oudolf, Hummelo, Holland **b.l.** Chenies Manor Garden, Bucks **b.c.** Wollerton Old Hall, Shropshire **br.** Country Living Garden, Chelsea 1995 ***d.*** Rupert Golby **p102 l.** ***d.*** Piet and Anja Oudolf, Hummelo, Holland **c.** ***d.*** Sue Berger, Bristol, Avon **r.** ***d.*** Piet and Anja Oudolf, Hummelo, Holland **p103 l.** The Old Vicarage, East Ruston, Norfolk ***d.*** Alan Gray and Graham Robeson **c.** The White House, Burpham, Sussex ***d.*** Elisabeth Woodhouse **r.** Country Living Garden, Chelsea 1995 ***d.*** Rupert Golby **p104 t.l.** ***d.*** Keeyla Meadows, San Francisco **t.r.** ***d.*** Keeyla Meadows, San Francisco **b.** The Castle Grounds, Guildford, Surrey **p105** Little Coopers, Eversley, Hants **p106 t.** The Sir Harold Hillier Gardens and Arboretum, Hants **c.t.** Lower House Farm, Gwent, Wales **c.** below The Picton Garden, Colwall, Worcs **b.** Eastgrove Cottage Garden, Sankyns Green, Worcs **p107** The Harcourt Arboretum, Nuneham Courtenay, Oxon **p108 t.** University Botanic Garden, Cambridge, Camb **b.** The Old Vicarage, East Ruston, Norfolk **p109 t.** The Dingle, Welshpool, Wales **b.** Hodsock Priory, Notts **p112** Butterstream, Trim, County Meath, Republic of Ireland **p113** Strybing Arboretum, San Francisco **p114** The Beth Chatto Gardens, Elmstead Market, Essex **p115 tl.** Coton Manor, Ravensthorpe, Northants **r.** The Beth Chatto Gardens, Elmstead Market, Essex **b.** Leonardslee, Sussex **p116 t.** La Mortola, Ventimiglia, Italy **b.** The Beth Chatto Gardens, Elmstead Market, Essex **p116-117** Strybing Arboretum, San Francisco **p117 r.** La Mortola, Ventimiglia, Italy **p119** ***d.*** Dan Pearson **p120 l.** Dartington Hall, Devon **inset** Benington Lordship, Herts **p120-121** North Springs, Sussex ***d.*** Anne Waring **p121 r.** Greystone Cottage, Oxon **p122 t.** Strybing Arboretum, San Francisco **l.** The Wildflower Centre, Austin, Texas **p123** Cerney House, Glos **inset** Strybing Arboretum, San Francisco **p124 l.** Ashtree Cottage, Wilts **p124-125** Little Coopers, Eversley, Hants **p125 t.** Coton Manor Gardens, Ravensthorpe, Northants **b.** Little Coopers, Eversley, Hants **p126 l.** Overbecks, Devon **p126 r.** ***d.*** James David, Austin, Texas **p128 l.** Coton Manor Gardens, Ravensthorpe, Northants **r.** Chiffchaffs, Bourton, Dorset **p128-129** Leonardslee, Sussex **p129 r.** Duckyls, Sharpthorne, West Sussex **p130** Mottisfont Abbey, Hants **inset** Butterstream, Trim, County Meath, Republic of Ireland **p131 l.** Little Court, Crawley, Hants **r.** Little Court, Crawley, Hants **p132** Huntington Botanical Garden, Los Angeles **p133** Eastgrove Cottage Garden and Nursery, Sankyns Green, Worcs. ***d.*** Malcolm and Carol Skinner **p134 t.** The Priory, Kemerton, Worcs **b.** Coates Manor, Sussex **p135 t.** White Windows, Longparish, Hants **b.** York Gate, Leeds, Yorkshire **p136** Ashtree Cottage, Wilts **p137 t.l.** Eastgrove Cottage Garden and Nursery, Sankyns Green, Worcs **tr.** Eastgrove Cottage Garden and Nursery, Sankyns Green, Worcs **b.** White Windows, Longparish, Hants **p138** Bosvigo House, Truro, Cornwall ***d.*** Michael and Wendy Perry **p139 t.** Coton Manor Gardens, Ravensthorpe, Northants **b.** Chenies Manor, Bucks **p141** Eastgrove Cottage Garden and Nursery, Sankyns Green, Worcs ***d.*** Malcolm and Carol Skinner **p142 t.** Barnsley House, Glos **p142 b.** ***d.*** Pam Schwert and Sibylle Kreutzberger, Glos **p143** ***d.*** Pam Schwert and Sibylle Kreutzberger, Glos **p144 t.l.** Lower House Farm, Gwent, Wales **p144 c.** Chenies Manor, Bucks **r.** Eastgrove Cottage Garden and Nursery, Sankyns Green, Worcs ***d.*** Malcolm and Carol Skinner **p145** The Old Rectory, Burghfield, Berks **inset** The Old Rectory, Burghfield, Berks **p146 t.** East Lambrook Manor, Somerset **b.** East Lambrook Manor, Somerset **p150** Eastgrove Cottage Garden and Nursery, Sankyns Green, Worcs ***d.*** Malcolm and Carol Skinner **p151 t.l.** Wollerton Old Hall, Shropshire **c.** Wollerton Old Hall, Shropshire **r.** Vale End, Surrey **b.** Wollerton Old Hall, Shropshire **p153** The Priory, Kemerton, Worcs **p155** White Windows, Longparish, Hants